MW01015117

Free *From Stress to Success* DVD from Trivium Test Prep

Dear Customer,

Thank you for purchasing from Trivium Test Prep! Whether you're looking to join the military, get into college, or advance your career, we're honored to be a part of your journey.

To show our appreciation (and to help you relieve a little of that test-prep stress), we're offering a **FREE *From Stress to Success* DVD by Trivium Test Prep**. Our DVD includes 35 test preparation strategies that will help keep you calm and collected before and during your big exam. All we ask is that you email us your feedback and describe your experience with our product. Amazing, awful, or just so-so: we want to hear what you have to say!

To receive your **FREE *From Stress to Success* DVD**, please email us at 5star@triviumtestprep.com. Include "Free 5 Star" in the subject line and the following information in your email:

1. The title of the product you purchased.

2. Your rating from 1 – 5 (with 5 being the best).

3. Your feedback about the product, including how our materials helped you meet your goals and ways in which we can improve our products.

4. Your full name and shipping address so we can send your FREE *From Stress to Success* DVD.

If you have any questions or concerns please feel free to contact me directly.

Thank you, and good luck with your studies!

Alyssa Wagoner
Quality Control
alyssa.wagoner@triviumtestprep.com

Table of Contents

Introduction to the PTCB Certification Exam

The Rise of the Pharmacy Technician

Working in a pharmacy just isn't what it used to be. Being a pharmacist used to mean mixing and dispensing drugs; now, a pharmacy is responsible for counseling patients, monitoring potentially adverse chemical interactions within increasingly complicated medication regimens, complying with a byzantine labyrinth of federal and state laws, running a business on top of all of that – and much, much more.

Enter the pharmacy technician. One of the most in-demand jobs in America, and still growing quickly, a pharmacy technician is responsible for assuming some of the most time-consuming and resource-intensive jobs that have fallen on pharmacists' shoulders in recent years. Pharmacy technicians are responsible for, among other things, uncovering potential mistakes in directions or dosages, advising pharmacists about drug indications and interactions, management of stock, maintenance of medication and administration. The whole point of the pharmacy technician is to free up the pharmacist to concentrate on what matters most: Focusing on patients.

The PTCB Exam

As you know, a pharmacy technician needs a large amount of specialized training in order to effectively assist a pharmacist. For this reason, the Pharmacy Technician Certification Board in Washington, D.C. developed a curriculum and examination to ensure that all pharmacy technicians have a standardized base of knowledge regarding basic chemistry, pharmacology, dosages, calculations, inventory control and patient service. This examination is known as the Pharmacy Technician Certification Examination, or PTCE, but is also called, simply, the PTCB exam. If a pharmacy technician wants to work for very long in the industry, they have no choice but to study for and pass this crucial test.

Most pharmacy technicians get a period of on-the-job training in a working pharmacy while they study for the PTCB exam in order to experience the real-life application of the knowledge they're gaining. This book will assume that you, too, are working in a pharmacy and that you have access to a local library or bookstore with resources you will need to learn the ins and outs of your job. No book can cram all of the references you'll need into one tome without cracking the spine – there's a lot to learn! But this guide will ensure that you have the references, resources and knowledge you need in order to pass the first, basic PTCB exam that will enable you to stay on at the pharmacy you're at and continue to improve your craft.

How This Book Will Help

Before we even dive into the PTCB, we'll cover some basic studying strategies you can use to maximize your retention on test day (and in your day-to-day work thereafter.) After you've got those down, we'll get down to the information you'll need to learn in order to pass the PTCB exam.

The PTCB exam is comprised of three core components:

1. How to assist the pharmacist in serving patients
2. The maintenance of medications and inventory control systems
3. Pharmacy management and administration

This book will take you through a crash course in each of these three components, giving you pointers, tips, references and links that will fully prepare you for anything the PTCB (or your pharmacist) can throw at you. There are also some basic test-taking strategies that apply to all examinations which will help you prepare. Finally, at the end of this book, you'll find 60 questions that simulate those you'll find on the official PTCB exam, so you can get a little practice tackling the big test before you actually sit down to take it, and a list of helpful resources that you can use to deepen your understanding and galvanize your confidence.

You've chosen a profession that not only makes a lot of financial and economic sense, but one that is noble and honorable, as well. You're a professional in the medical field, and your hard work will directly affect the quality of life for thousands of people over the course of your career. The amount of work you put in now and in the future to become a great pharmacy technician won't just reflect in your test scores and your paychecks. You'll see it in the smiles of patients who are slowly but surely healing, in the relieved eyes of the mothers of sick children, and in the gracious, thankful words of the pharmacist who couldn't be half as successful in his or her mission without your hard efforts. Your career as a pharmacy tech starts here – with the PTCB exam. If no one else has thanked you for choosing this demanding and crucial line of work, let us be the first to do so: Thank you, and best of luck.

Basic Studying Strategies

A lot of folks never get the 101 of how to study. In the age of standardized testing, studying has become about the memorization of facts, rather than gaining deep knowledge of concepts and the ability to synthesize disparate pieces of information. In the interest of best preparing you for the PTCB exam, here are some basic studying strategies that will help you make the most of the time you spend poring over the books.

Get Motivated and Stay Motivated

Easier said than done, right? But there are definite approaches you can take to studying that will help you gain motivation and – most crucially – maintain it throughout the sometimes arduous task of studying.

1. *Get your motivation.* You need to know what it is you want and focus squarely on that as your motivation. Have you ever heard the old saying "Keep your eyes on the prize?" It is singular focus that will help you get motivated to study and keep studying even when Facebook, television, and texts from friends out at the bar having fun without you start singing their siren song at you. You know what you want – to pass the PTCB exam. So you need to make that your number one priority. Make it real. Schedule it and pay for it well ahead of time. Figure out exactly what you need to study and for how long in order to pass it. If you need to envision all of the great rewards that will come to you *after* you've passed the exam, do that. You've already taken a crucial first step by cracking open this book; keep it up! Remember that right now, passing the PTCB exam is your job. You wouldn't skip out on a shift at work, and you shouldn't skip out on a shift studying. Set a schedule and skip to it.

2. *Invest in the PTCB exam.* A lot of employers will pay the fees required to take the exam, which can leave some test-takers without a strong sense of investment in their success. Create your own investment! Buy your own books, designate a suitable place in your home or at the library to study, and keep your study materials on hand with you in case you get some unexpected free time.

3. *Manage your distractions.* Most distractions come from – you! It's true. Hey, all of your friends might be playing Xbox or throwing a party or watching the latest episode of *Game of Thrones*, but no one is holding you down and making you break focus from your studies. Don't give in, and whenever possible, remove yourself from the narrow occasion of distraction. If you're having a hard time concentrating on your studies, take a deep breath and look inside at what it is that's bothering you, then take clear, actionable steps to get rid of it.

4. *Set short-term, achievable goals.* Don't sit down and say, "I'm going to study tonight." Analyze what you have to do. What do you want to achieve in the amount of time you have allotted for studying? Are you weakest on drug interactions? Calculations? Identify what you need to achieve and set an actionable, measurable plan to make it happen. When it's crunch time, you know you can kick things into high gear and accomplish an entire day's work in just a couple of hours – work shifts to fit the amount of time you have, not the other way around. So make sure you're setting clearly defined time periods to study specific areas of the test you know you need to learn.

Concentrate

It's hard to stay focused! But follow this handy mini-guide, and you'll find that your active studying yields a lot more gain in much less time.

1. *Create a good environment for studying.* Set aside an area that is only for studying, and keep it that way. Make sure it's well-stocked with everything you need to study (and maybe a mini-fridge, too, for snacks) and that it's quiet, but not too relaxing. Remember, when you're studying, you're working!

2. *Study at the right time.* During the day and early evening are the best times to study, because you'll retain more information. Try to have as few competing activities going on at the same time, and ensure you're taking regular breaks. When you start feeling tired or you can't concentrate, it's time to take a break or quit altogether.

3. *Keep your concentration.* It's probably some kind of law of the universe — the minute you sit down to study, your brain suddenly remembers all of the errands you have to run, the people you have to call and the bills you have to pay. Make sure you've got a pen and paper nearby to jot down any thoughts that pop up while you're studying, regardless of whether they're related to your studies or not. By "capturing" them on paper, your brain will more easily return to your studies, even if you've gone a little off-track. Then, when you're finished studying, make sure to attend to the things you've written down! You don't want them creeping back up during the next study session and causing you anxiety.

Retain What You Learn

You can spend all the time in the world skimming through book after book that you think will help prepare you for the PTCB exam, but if you don't take the time to slow down, reflect, clarify and restate the new knowledge you've got, you're simply not going to retain what you need to pass the test.

Here are the five major reasons people forget what they've learned. Avoid these at all costs! You don't want your precious study time to go down the drain.

1. *You just didn't learn the material well enough.* It's not enough to simply read something. You've got to forcibly impress new wrinkles on your brain by giving it the necessary attention and interest it needs to make the knowledge permanent. As you read, take small breaks and review what you've learned. It helps to create notes and flash cards as you go along to make these intervals more productive.

2. *You think of yourself as a forgetful person or a bad test-taker or studier.* If you've got a negative image of yourself, you're going to make it a reality. Negative self-concept is one of the most powerful obstacles people face on a day-to-day basis. Have you ever heard someone say, "I'm just not good at math?" That's not true – *everyone* is good at math. Our brains are built to abstract and calculate – it's the reason we have air conditioning, airplanes and iPhones and the chimpanzees are still swinging in the trees. But when people tell themselves they're bad at something, they release themselves from accountability for their poor performance. If you think you're just bad at taking tests, or just bad at studying, you're going to be. Instead, tell yourself that you're just as good as the next person at studying – because it's true! No one has any magic predilection or brain wiring that you lack. It's all about your attitude and the amount of work you're willing to put in.

3. *You don't use it, so you lose it.* Your brain works hard to keep important information front-and-center. In order to do this, it's got to release detailed memories that aren't relevant to the situation at hand. While studying for the PTCB exam, you've got to set up a regular, scheduled regimen and review what you've learned often, or the information you've read will flap out of your head before you even get a chance to take the test. Use it or lose it!

4. *You're distracted.* Disuse, as mentioned above, is a pretty powerful obstacle to remembering what you need. But an even more powerful obstacle is distraction: Emotions, misplaced concentration, interference and anxiety can make it very difficult to retain what you need in order to pass the PTCB exam. When you're studying, do your best to limit your intake of information from other sources. Yes, your favorite blog will still be there when you're done studying for this test – but if you're reading every post every day like you usually do, you're actually actively interfering with your brain's process of storing what you've studied for later retention.

Chapter 1: Assisting the Pharmacist in Serving Patients

Here we go! This is the first and largest portion of the PTCB exam – in fact, it comprises almost two-thirds of the entire quiz. So when you're studying, make sure you've got this part down pat!

Define the terms prescription and medication order.

Prescriptions and medication orders serve essentially the same purpose: They are a means of communication between a prescriber (usually a physician) and a medication dispenser (usually a pharmacist.)

A medication order is a written request from a prescriber or a transcription of a verbal or telephone order in an inpatient facility. You'll typically see medication orders if you go to work for a hospital pharmacy.

A prescription is a written request from a prescriber or a transcription of a verbal or telephone order in outpatient (or ambulatory) facility. You'll typically see prescriptions in retail pharmacies, where medications are dispensed to patients who are self-administering at home.

Define some of the most common pharmacy terms associated with prescriptions and medication orders.

Generic names are nomenclature for drugs, medications and other chemical compounds that don't change, regardless of how pharmaceutical companies have branded them.

Brand names are trademarks used by pharmaceutical companies to identify their particular medication formulations.

Legend drugs are medications that must be prescribed by someone with prescription authority, such as a physician, physician's assistant, or nurse practitioner, and must be dispensed by legally qualified pharmacies.

Over-the-counter drugs can be purchased without a prescription as long as they are properly labeled for home use.

There is a formulary is in every pharmacy, but what it is differs slightly depending on whether you're working in a hospital or a retail pharmacy. In a hospital, a formulary is a list of drugs that the pharmacy stocks that are available to resident prescribers. In a retail pharmacy, formularies are usually lists of drugs that are or are not covered under different health insurance benefit plans.

Common abbreviations in use in pharmacies today.

There are a lot of abbreviations (also known as "sig codes") used in in prescriptions and medication orders that are mostly based on Latin. Lowercase Roman numerals usually denote a quantity, such as the number of capsules or tablets to take. (We'll cover how to read Roman numerals later in the book.)

Other abbreviations include *x-substitutions*, which is where the widely-recognized *Rx* (meaning "prescription") belongs. Within this subset, you'll also find *dx* (meaning "diagnosis") and *sx* (meaning "symptoms.")

Hasty or sloppy abbreviating can lead to major errors, so use caution with them. The word "units" is never abbreviated to the letter "U," for instance, because writing a "U" too quickly can look like a zero, which could lead to a potentially fatal dosing error. Never use a "U" in abbreviations for prescriptions or medication orders, and if you see that someone has used it, check and double-check with your pharmacist and fellow technicians to be sure you're reading the abbreviation correctly. Other characters you should use extra caution with if they appear within an abbreviation are *q., qid,* and *qod,* because they can be hard to distinguish from one another.

Here is a table of of the most common pharmacy abbreviations you'll run into on the PTCB exam:

Abbrev.,	Meaning	Abbrev.	Meaning	Abbrev.	Meaning
AA	OF EACH	KG	KILOGRAM	qAM	EVERY MORNING
AC	BEFORE A MEAL	L	LITER	qD	EVERY DAY
AD	RIGHT EAR	LB	POUND	qH	EVERY HOUR
AS	LEFT EAR	ML	MILLILITER	qHS	EVERY BEDTIME
AU	BOTH EARS	NG	NASO GASTRIC	QID	FOUR A DAY
BID	TWICE A DAY	OD	RIGHT EYE	qMO	EVERY MONTH
BUCCAL	CHEEK/GUM	OS	LEFT EYE	qOD	EVERY OTHER DAY
C	WITH	OU	BOTH EYES	qPM	EVERY EVENING
CAP	CAPSULE	OZ	OUNCE	QS	QUANTITY SUFFICIENT
G	GALLON	PC	AFTER A MEAL	qWK	EVERY WEEK
GM	GRAM	PO	ORALLY	SL	SUB-LINGUAL
GTT	DROP	PR	RECTALLY	SQ	SUB-CUTANEOUS
HS	AT BEDTIME	PRN	AS NEEDED	STAT	IMMEDIATELY
IC	INTRA CARDIAC	PV	VAGINALLY	TDS	3 TIMES A DAY
IM	INTRA MUSCULAR	q	EVERY	TID	THREE A DAY

INJ	INJECTION	q__°	EVERY__HOURS	TSP	TEASPOON
IV	INTRAVENOUS	q__H	EVERY__HOURS	UD	AS DIRECTED

Identify the elements of a medication order

In a perfect world, every medication order will be fully filled out, free of errors and have as much information as possible. Of course, this is the real world, and the rapid, high-stress pace of most hospitals makes it difficult for doctors to fill out a perfect medication order every time. As far as the PTCB exam is concerned, this is the information that belongs on a medication order – just be aware that you might not always get all of this in a real-life situation!

- The name of the patient
- The hospital identification number
- The location of the patient's room and bed
- The generic drug name if available
- The brand name (if specific product is needed, or no generic exists)
- The route of administration
- The site of administration (if needed)
- The dosage form
- The dose and strength
- The frequency and duration of administration (if needed)
- The rate and time of administration (if needed)
- Indication for use of medication
- Other instructions (if needed)
- Name, signature and credentials of prescriber or person ordering medication
- Date and time of the order

Upon receiving a new medication order, the first thing a pharmacy technician needs to do is verify its clarity and level of completion. If there is any information missing, it's up to you to try to get that info without bothering your pharmacist (if possible and allowed.)

Once you've decided that the medication order is clear and complete, you'll need to prioritize it among all the other orders that have come in according to its urgency. The medications that are needed the most are the ones that need to be filled first. You can evaluate the urgency of a medication order by checking the route, time of administration, type of medication, intended use of the medication, and any patient-specific circumstances on the form.

Processing the Medication Order in the Computer

In order to process the medication order in the computer, you're going to need to accomplish a few different steps:

1. Positively identify the patient (so as not to send a patient the wrong drugs.)

2. Compare the medication order with the patient's current medication profile (or, if there is no current medication profile, create one.) Look for duplications or other potential issues. This is a good place to do a cursory scan of the medication order to ensure that it makes sense in regard to other information on the patient's profile, such as their age, allergies and current medication prescriptions.

3. Enter the drug into the system. In order to do this, you are going to need to know both brand names and generic names, although your computer probably has a search function for this. You will also need to know those abbreviations! If you are ever unsure about a drug name or an abbreviation, always check and double check with a fellow technician or the pharmacist. It's better to be safe than sorry, so never make assumptions when it comes to interpreting medical orders! Many computer systems

have safeguards in place to prevent medication orders that interfere with other drugs or a patient's allergies, and that send out alerts if there is a dosage error, but you cannot rely on the computer to do the work for you. Each patient's situation is going to be unique, so each medication order requires human judgment. If the computer ever alerts you, you have to check with the pharmacist to be sure you are interpreting the medication order correctly.

4. Verify that you have entered the correct dose.

5. Enter the schedule of administration. Most hospitals have standard medication administration times that revolve around therapeutic issues, nursing schedules or coordinated services. If you're unclear about the hospital's standard schedule of administration, check the policy on file or ask a fellow technician or your pharmacist.

6. Enter any comments in the *clinical comments* field. It's imperative that a prescriber's directions to the patient are conveyed clearly and accurately. If there are additional comments for a caregiver, this is also the place to put them. Other information to be transcribed here would be anything nurses need to know, or any additional information a pharmacist may need in the future.

7. Verify that the prescriber's name is entered correctly.

8. Fill and label the medication. After you've generated the label, you'll need to put the right quantity of the right medication in the chosen receptacle. This is the time to review and review and review to make sure the label, the order and the product are all correct. This is your last chance to catch an error before sending the medication to a pharmacist for the final check!

Receive and process prescriptions in an outpatient pharmacy

The first step in receiving and processing a patient's prescription in an outpatient pharmacy is identifying the patient. If you've served this patient before, you'll need to get an identifying piece of information from them, such as their date of birth, address or phone number to confirm their identity. If you've never served the patient before, you'll need to get the following information from them:

- Their name (be sure it's spelled correctly!)
- Their address
- Their phone number
- Their insurance information (ask them for their insurance card to ensure you get it right the first time)
- Their date of birth
- Their drug allergies
- Their current prescriptions and over-the-counter medications, including vitamins and health supplements
- Their significant health conditions

You are allowed to receive prescriptions from the patient if they have a paper copy in hand, or from the prescriber of the medication over the phone, by fax or through a secure electronic transmission. Many pharmacies have web pages that can process refill requests, as well.

It's important to get information on who will be paying for the prescription. You'll need to know who will be the primary payer for the prescription, how much the patient will need to pay (if their insurance requires a copay) and sometimes, you'll need the drug formulary as well.

When you're getting ready to check a prescription for clarity and completeness, it's almost identical to the process for checking a medication order. Here are the elements you'll usually find on a given prescription:

- The patient's name

- The patient's home address
- The date the prescription was written
- The name of the drug (either generic or brand name)
- The strength of the drug and the dose to be administered
- The route of administration
- The frequency
- The duration of use
- The quantity you'll dispense
- The number of refills allowed (if any)
- The substitution authority (or refusal, if applicable)
- The signature and credentials of the prescriber
- The DEA number (if necessary)
- The reason for use or indication (though this isn't generally required)
- Whether a prescription is DAW (meaning "Dispense as Written") or if a generic can be substituted.

Assess the authenticity of an order

It's sad, but true – sometimes people will attempt to forge a prescription, particularly for controlled substances. It's part of your job to screen prescriptions for anything that looks out of the ordinary. Here's a list of things to look for that may indicate a potential forgery:

- A dispensation quantity that's out of the ordinary, or looks higher than a prescriber would normally prescribe
- An unusual signature
- Any signs of erasure (such as with white-out) or any overwriting of the strength or quantity of a drug (such as turning a "0" into an "8")
- An invalid DEA number

Every prescription has a DEA number to help you verify that it's authentic. A valid DEA number will always consist of two letters and seven numbers.

If the holder of the DEA number is a registrant (like a doctor or a pharmacy) the first letter will always be an "A" or a "B." If the holder is a mid-level practitioner (like a nurse practitioner) the first letter will always be an "M." The second letter is always related to the holder's name – for instance, if the registrant is a physician, the second letter of their DEA number will always be the first letter of their last name.

The seven numbers have special significance, as well. The first, third and fifth numbers are called the odd group, and the second, fourth and sixth numbers are called the even group. The seventh number is always the last number of the sum of the odd group and double the sum of the even group.

Here is the equation, for those of you mathematically inclined: $x + y(2) = z$

Where:

x = the sum of the odd group
y = the sum of the even group

solve for z, and the last numeral of z will be the final, seventh character in the DEA number.

All of that information can be a little difficult to visualize, so here's a detailed breakdown:

The writer of the prescription is Dr. Janelle Malkin, M.D. Her hypothetical DEA number is A M 1 2 7 9 7 6 9.

A	M	1	2	7	9	7	6	9
(*1)	(*2)	(*3)	(*4)	(*3)	(*4)	(*3)	(*4)	(*5)

(*1)Identifies the registrant/holder's credentials

(*2) Identifies the first letter of the registrant/holder's last name

(*3) The "odd group"

(*4) The "even group"

(*5) The last numeral of the sum of the odd group plus the sum of the even group times two

To properly understand how to arrive at this number, we need to use the equation from earlier. We simply plug in the values to arrive at our conclusion:

$x + y(2) = z$

The sum of the odd group is 15, so we'll use that in place of x.

$15 + y(2) = z$

The sum of the even group is 17, so we'll use that in place of y.

$15 + 17(2) = z$

Since we double the value of y, we reduce the equation down to this:

$15 + 34 = z$

And now we know that $z = 49$.

$15 + 34 = 49$.

Since 9 is the last numeral of 49, it is also the seventh numeral in the DEA number.

Processing a Prescription in the Computer

In order to process the prescription in the computer, you're going to need to accomplish a few steps that look an awful lot like those you need to complete medication order – with just a few differences:

1. Once you have located or created the patient's profile, verify their identity.

2. Enter or verify their third-party billing information (this is usually their health insurance.)

3. Compare the medication order with the patient's current medication profile. Look for duplications or other potential issues. Again, perform a cursory scan of the prescription to ensure that it makes sense in regard to other information, such as their age, allergies and current medication prescriptions.

4. Enter the prescription. The information required in this step varies from system to system, but you'll usually need to fill in the following elements:
   - The name of the prescriber
   - Any directions for use or special comments
   - The quantity to be filled
   - The initials of the pharmacist performing the final check on the prescription
   - The number of refills allowed (if any)

5. Check for any error messages that may come up. These are some of the most common:

- REFILL TOO SOON: Usually, insurance companies allow patients a 30-day supply of medications. If a patient tries to get a refill too soon, this warning will pop up.

- DRUG-DRUG or DRUG-ALLERGY INTERACTION: If the software catches a potential adverse reaction or bad drug interaction, it will alert you. Some systems don't just let you know if there's an interaction – they'll also let you know the potential severity of the interaction. If you get this message, let the pharmacist know right away.

- NONFORMULARY/DRUG NOT COVERED: Many insurers have lists of drugs that they're willing to pay for. If a drug isn't on the list, the third party won't pay for it. If you get this message, inform your pharmacist.

- MISSING/INVALID ID: If you get this message, the patient may not be enrolled in their indicated insurance program. If you get this message, go back and double-check whether you entered all of the patient's information correctly.

6. Fill and label the medication. After you have generated the label, you will need to put the right quantity of the right medication in the chosen receptacle. This is the time to review as many times as you need to feel confident that the label, the order and the product are all correct. In general, these components need to appear on a prescription label:

- The name of the patient
- The date the prescription is being filled (or refilled)
- The name of the prescriber
- The prescription number (sequential)

- The name of the drug (if it's a generic, you need to put in the name of manufacturer
- The quantity to be dispensed
- The directions for the patient on how to use
- The number of refills allowed (if applicable.)

It's important to note that, unlike a medication order, it's never okay to use abbreviations or pharmaceutical shorthand on a label intended for a patient who will use the medication at home. In fact, there should be auxiliary information on the label that makes it *more clear* to the untrained patient about how to take their medications. When you're filling out a label with instructions for a patient on how to use the medication at home, it needs to include (at a bare minimum) the following set of pieces of information:

- Directions for administration
- How many units make up one dose (for instance, two capsules)
- The route of administration
- How frequently to take the medication, or at what time of day the patient should take it
- How long the patient should take the medication, if applicable (this is especially important in the case of antibiotics)
- The indication of purpose, if necessary.

Ultimately, it's the pharmacist's job to make sure every patient clearly understands how to take the medication they've been dispensed. But since your job is assisting the pharmacist with this action, you'll sometimes be called upon to fulfill this duty.

Identify and use NDC numbers correctly.

Drug manufacturers use something called NDC numbers to identify their drugs – they are all specific on a product-by-product basis, and are used to verify that pharmacists and technicians are using the right medication to fill a prescription, and for verification for third-party payers like insurance companies.

An NDC number is usually ten numerals with a few hyphens thrown in for good measure. A typical NDC number may look like this:

0391-5428-11

88362-411-77

48394-7888-6

Here's how they work:

- The first group of numerals are the number specific to the manufacturer who creates the medication. All medications made by a specific manufacturer will have the same first group of numerals.
- The second group of numerals represents the specific product. This will be different for every product.
- The third group of numerals represents the size of the package.

This is where NDC numbers get confusing: Most of the time, when you're communicating an NDC number to a third party, you've got to transmit them in a 5-4-2 configuration, even though the original NDC number might have a different hyphen format. This is because most insurance companies' computers won't read an NDC number that is out of the 5-4-2 format, and if it's not formatted correctly, it could result in an erroneous payment (or no payment at all!

Shifting an NDC number into the 5-4-2 format is not terribly difficult, but it's highly specific. Basically, you have to look at the current format of the numbers. Is it in 4-4-2? 4-3-3? 5-5-1? Then, whichever group of numerals is *not* in the correct format gets a zero at the beginning. So let's take that first group of NDC numbers we looked at and correct them to get them ready for transmission to a third-party payer's computer system:

0391-5428-11 – this is a 4-4-2 format, and we need it to be 5-4-2. So we know that the first group of numerals is incorrect! Thus, we put a zero at the beginning of the first group of numerals, and the new number we get is 00391-5428-11.

88362-411-77 – this is a 5-3-2 format, so we need to put a zero at the beginning of the second group of numerals to get 88362-0411-77

48394-7888-6 – this is a 5-4-1 format, so we need to fix the last group of numerals with a zero at the beginning, yielding the number 4839-7888-06.

Fairly simple, but without the right knowledge, it can be difficult!

Counseling Patients and Receiving Pay for Services/Products

Once you've completed a prescription for a patient, you'll need to ring them up at the register and receive payment. This is a four-step process:

1. First, you have to ensure that the patient's name and other information is correct, so you don't accidentally give medication to the wrong person.
2. Because a lot of patients have questions, they have a right to be counseled by the pharmacist. But it's not up to them to bring it up to you – you are legally obligated to offer them counseling.
3. If your pharmacy has never served this particular patient, it's a requirement of the Health Insurance Portability and Accountability Act (also known as HIPAA) that you provide them literature regarding your organization's patient privacy policy.
4. Upon receiving the privacy information required by HIPAA, the patient needs to sign to verify. If you offer them pharmacist counseling and they

refuse to take it, they may also need to sign (though this depends on state requirements and policies by certain third-party payers.)

Transferring Prescriptions

There are a lot of laws and regulations that cover the transfer of prescriptions, depending on which state you're practicing in and what class of drug is involved in the transfer. It's important to understand that it's the pharmacist's responsibility to ensure all information is transferred correctly – regardless of what laws or regulations are involved. The buck also stops with pharmacists when it comes to prescription transfers that the pharmacy is accepting. You, as the technician, will likely be the one doing the transferring or receiving, but if something goes wrong, it's going to come back around on the pharmacist's head – so be sure you do it right, every time.

When you receive a transfer from another pharmacy, you've got to get as much information as you are able to about the prescription – even if the other party isn't offering it up. You've at least got to secure the patient's name and the name of the pharmacy where the prescription is coming from, but you may need other information as well, such as the number of refills that are authorized. If a patient brings in an empty container, you can examine the label to help collect information for the transfer.

Restricted-Use Medications

Not every drug is allowed to be dispensed in every facility. For instance, typical retail pharmacies have much broader restrictions on what they can hand out than hospitals – this is because some drugs have highly specific warnings and precautions that need to be taken.

The Food and Drug Administration (FDA) is the regulatory agency in charge of making these determinations. When they decide that the potential risks of a drug outweigh its potential benefits, they require a pharmacy to perform an REMS, which stands for Risk Evaluation and Mitigation Strategy. If the FDA decides that a drug is safe for dispensation without an REMS, but they still have substantial reservations, they may require that all prescriptions for that drug be accompanied by something called a Medication Guide. Medication Guides have information the FDA wants patients to know to help them avoid potentially serious side effects and to perform the administration of their medication correctly.

Investigational Medications

Sometimes, your pharmacy will participate in a drug study that is investigating the effectiveness and safety of certain medications which have yet to be approved for full distribution. In order for the drug study to be successful, you as the pharmacy technician will need to ensure that certain practices are followed and conditions are met – though they'll vary for each drug, depending on its intended use and chemical composition, you're generally responsible for the following:

- Correctly storing the drug
- Keeping correct, complete records
- Performing rigorous inventory control
- Preparing the medications correctly
- Dispensing the medications correctly
- Properly labeling all drugs that are part of an investigational study

An Overview of Drug Information

One of the most important parts of your task in assisting the pharmacist is knowing as much information about specific drugs as possible. You need to be able to know how to handle drugs, what the availability of certain medications is, and the uses of many different drugs. While it's the pharmacist's job to counsel patients, there are many questions patients will ask that are within your power (and job description) to answer, so you need to have a good grasp of this material! Of course, you'll always have your references available, and it's important to consult them (or the pharmacist) to make sure you're giving the best answer you can possible give.

Questions You Are Legally Allowed to Answer

Before we even get started, however, let's draw a bright line between the questions you're allowed to answer and the questions that only a pharmacist is legally allowed to answer. There are seven kinds of questions you're allowed to answer:

1. *Questions about general drug information.* These include, but are not necessarily limited to, questions about:

    - The generic names for brand-name medications
    - The brand names for generic medications
    - The active ingredients in brand name medications
    - The manufacturers of a drug
    - Whether a patent has expired on a drug
    - If there is a generic form of a drug in existence
    - If a medication is a legend drug or an over-the-counter drug

2. *Questions about the availability and cost of a drug.* These questions pertain to:

    - The different dosage forms of a medication that your pharmacy makes available
    - Whether a drug is available in liquids, capsules, powders, etc.
    - The sizes available
    - The concentrations available
    - The prices of a brand-name drug
    - The prices of a generic drug
    - Any potential shortages or gaps in availability in the national supply chain

3. *Questions about how a drug should be stored, or the stability of a particular medication.* These include, but aren't limited to:
   - Whether a drug needs to be refrigerated
   - General questions about how long a drug is stable in different storage containers, such as a vial, ampule or syringe

4. *Questions about mathematical calculations.* It's not patients' job to do mathematical calculations and conversions – it's your job to break it all down for them as simply and neatly as possible to reduce the chances that they'll make a mistake when self-administering medications. These questions include:
   - Conversions from the metric system to avoirdupois (for instance, how many liters are in a gallon, or how many milliliters are in an ounce.)

5. *Questions about how a drug is prepared.* These are rare questions, but you may encounter them from patients who need to perform special preparations on drugs at home, or get them from a particularly inquisitive patient. They include:
   - How particular drugs need to be reconstituted (some drugs are less stable in liquid form, and are dispensed as powders to be reconstituted at the time of administration.)

6. *Questions regarding laws and regulations that pertain to a pharmacy.* These are questions regarding:
   - Whether a drug is a controlled substance
   - What schedule a controlled substance is classified under
   - The processes and procedures for transferring prescriptions

7. *Questions regarding miscellaneous information.* Be careful here – "miscellaneous" means a lot of different things to a lot of different people. If you're ever in doubt as to whether you're allowed to answer a question, always defer to the pharmacist. Don't be afraid to ask for help! However, on the PTCB exam, "miscellaneous" questions refer to:

   - How to find drug information
   - Web addresses or phone numbers for manufacturers
   - Patent expiration dates
   - How to order reference materials

Questions Only a Pharmacist Can Answer

These are the questions that only pharmacists are legally qualified to give an answer to. They include, but are not limited to:

1. *Questions about alternative therapies.* Any question that requires clinical knowledge has to be answered by a pharmacist. Questions like this might pertain to:

   - Drugs available outside the United States and their potential equivalents
   - Drugs that may work as an alternative to another medication
   - Supplements or over-the-counter medications that may interact with or be complementary to a prescribed drug

2. *Questions about drug allergies.* It's your job to know a lot about drug allergies, and to be able to identify if a patient is allergic to a medication, but if a patient asks a question regarding allergies, a pharmacist needs to use their clinical judgment. Questions like this might be about:

   - Drugs that are safe to use for people with specific allergies
   - Specific allergies and their potential drug interactions
   - Symptoms of drug allergies

3. *Questions about the dose or the administration of a drug.* These questions might cover:

   - The standard or typical dosage for a medication
   - The standard or typical duration of treatment regarding a specific medication
   - Strengths and weaknesses of different kinds of administration

4. *Questions about drug compatibility or interactions.* These questions require a specialized knowledge of doses, concentrations and other clinical information, so a pharmacist will need to handle questions concerning:

   - Compatibility of legend drugs
   - Compatibility of legend drugs with over-the-counter medications
   - Compatibility of legend drugs with food
   - Compatibility of over-the-counter medications with food
   - Compatibility of legend drugs with supplements
   - Compatibility of over-the-counter medications with supplements
   - Potential interactions with legend drugs
   - Potential interactions between legend drugs and over-the-counter medications
   - Potential interactions between legend drugs and food
   - Potential interactions between legend drugs and supplements

- Potential interactions between over-the-counter medications and food
- Potential interactions between over-the-counter medications and supplements

5. *Questions about side effects.* These might include questions about:
   - The specific side effects of a drug
   - Any adverse side effect of a drug
   - Potential adverse side effects of mixing drugs, food, or supplements
   - Whether a drug can cause a specific side effect

6. *Questions concerning pregnant or nursing mothers.* This requires clinical knowledge, so a pharmacist has to answer all questions concerning:
   - The safety of a drug for pregnant or nursing mothers
   - The effect of a drug on pregnant or nursing mothers
   - The effect of a drug on a zygote or fetus

7. *Questions concerning non-FDA approved uses.* These might concern:
   - Whether a drug meant to treat one condition is safe to treat another
   - Whether a drug approved for another condition may soon be approved for another
   - Whether a drug not approved for treatment a specific condition will be safe or effective

References for Drug Information

There are three types of references concerning drug information:

1. *Primary.* These are highly technical, original research articles published in scientific journals. To be able to read these articles, you typically require a familiarity with current research in the field, a specialized degree of technical knowledge and the ability to assess the methodology of a study. Pharmacy technicians aren't expected to consult or use primary references when they're seeking out drug information for patients.

2. *Secondary.* These are generally indexes of scholarly articles that are used when pharmacists need the most current and up-to-date information on a particular topic. These are most often consulted when you can't find what you're looking for anywhere else. Pharmacy technicians usually aren't expected to consult or use secondary references.

3. *Tertiary.* This is the most common type of reference that both you and the pharmacist will use on a day-to-day basis. Read on to the next section for an overview of these.

Common References

The table on the next page contains some of the most common references you'll find in a pharmacy.

What It's Called:	What It Contains:	Who Publishes It:
American Drug Index	An alphabetized index of drugs containing information on generic names, brand names, chemical names, manufacturers and more.	Facts and Comparisons
Mosby's Drug Consult	A general drug information guide organized by generic drug names. Provides complete monographs and is considered to be one of the most comprehensive references available.	Elsevier Science
The Physician's Desk Reference	Contains the package inserts for drugs from most manufacturers. Gives information on effects, indications, interactions, dosing and more. This guide is not comprehensive and only has information about certain brand-name drugs.	Thomson Medical Economics
Drug Facts and Comparisons	Available in print and online (where it is regularly updated) it provides complete drug monographs on a comprehensive array of medications, organized by therapeutic class.	Wolters Kluwers Health
USPDI	The United States Pharmacopeia Drug Information is a reference that comes in three volumes and gives medication information not just to	Thomson

| | pharmacists, but to many other health care professionals, as well. It also provides comprehensive information regarding drug laws and regulations. | |

Specialized References

The table on this page contains references that are used for specific functions and purposes, and will usually be used primarily by pharmacists.

What It's Called:	What It Contains:	Who Publishes It:
Pharmacist's Pharmacopeia	Instructions on Compounding 101, as well as all official standards for strength, quality and purity of compounded substances. Procedures to ensure the standards are met, and information regarding compounding, storage, labeling and packaging of compounded medications. Food ingredients, colorings, preservatives and more. Also provides applicable information on the laws and regulations concerning compounding.	U.S. Pharmacopeia
Extended Stability of Parenteral Drugs	Data on the stability of IV solutions that are stored longer than 24 hours.	American Society of Health-System Pharmacists (ASHP)
Red Book	Prices for legend and over-the-counter	Medical Economics

	medications, as well as supplies and equipment for the pharmacy and patients. Also contains NDC numbers and therapeutic equivalences that are approved in the FDA's *Orange Book,* a book that lists all of the FDA's approved drugs and therapeutic and bioequivalent. Also lists information such as products free of sugar or allergens like lactose and sulfites.	
Natural Medicines Comprehensive Database	An index of natural medicines, including herbs, supplements and potential food interactions. Available in print and online.	Therapeutic Research Facility

Using the Internet to Look Up Drug Information

The Internet is one of the greatest inventions in human history – it puts unfathomable amounts of information at our fingertips instantly. The problem is that many people are using the Internet without checking and double-checking that the source is correct, trustworthy and up-to-date. Many patients are researching disreputable resources for information about their conditions or the drugs they're taking, and as a pharmacy technician, you may end up fielding a lot of questions based on people's misinterpretations.

As a pharmacy technician, you've got to be sure that any Internet source you use to compile drug information for a patient is reputable, current and accurate. In general, you can trust web sites that belong to the government and major medical organizations, but you still need to know whether that site is up-to-date!

Here is a list of web sites with drug information that you can trust:

1. www.pharmacist.com. This is the page that belongs to the American Pharmacists' Association, and is home to an array of helpful information for both pharmacists and pharmacy technicians

2. www.pharmacy.org. The home page of the Virtual Library Pharmacy, which has links and information about manufacturers, hospitals, journals, references, pharmacy associations and much more.

3. www.ashp.org. This page belongs to the American Society of Health-System Pharmacists, and also has a lot of good information for professionals working in a pharmacy.

4. www.ashp.org/shortage. A very useful site that gives information on chemical shortages in the United States, what products are affected, potential alternatives and an estimate on how long it will take for the shortage to be alleviated.

5. www.ismp.org. The Institute for Safe Medication Practices maintains this web site, which is a resource that contains information on medication errors, strategies for preventing them and mechanisms for reporting them.

6. www.fda.gov. The home page for the Food and Drug Administration.

7. www.fda.gov/cder. The home page for the FDA's Center for Drug Evaluation and Research. This is where the FDA lists links and information for professionals regarding drugs, such as which new drugs the agency has approved, if there are any shortages in particular regions or nationwide, safety information, and bioequivalents for generic drugs. This is what is known as the *Orange Book.*

8. www.cdc.gov. This is the page maintained be the Centers for Disease Control and Prevention, and it hosts a lot of useful information about diseases, vaccines, health tips for travelers and more.

Best Practices for Compounding Medications

The actual act of compounding chemicals in order to make drugs is governed by the boards of pharmacy state to state, although the chemicals themselves are approved (or disapproved) by the FDA, which still follows the guidelines set forth in the now-defunct Food and Drug Modernization Act of 1997.

This is a very large and information-intensive portion of the PTCB, so we're going to cover it in minute detail. There are nine important elements of the best practices for compounding:

1. *Patient Counseling.* Regardless of whether a drug is compounded or not, patients need to be offered counseling on how to correctly use it. Because compounded drugs often have differences in the way they should be used, stored or handled, it's especially important to inform patients of any special considerations involved in taking a compounded medication. Always let your pharmacist know when you're dispensing a compounded medication so they can properly counsel a patient.

2. *The compounder's responsibilities.* The compounder is in charge of (and accountable for) every element of the compounding process, including ensuring that all personnel are trained properly.

3. *The compounding environment.* Any space where medication is being compounded should have plenty of room for equipment and any necessary support materials. It needs to be kept as clean as possible to prevent potential contamination of one drug by another, and temperature and light

must also be controlled for, since some chemicals are sensitive to these considerations. Lastly, a compounding area needs to have a sink with both hot and cold water, so that compounders can wash their hands and clean their equipment.

4. *The stability of compounded preparations.* Chemicals can break down or change over time – and many of them will change too quickly (or improperly) if certain precautions aren't taken. It's important that compounded medications have the same properties when the patient is taking them that they had when you first compounded them. In order to ensure this is the case, you'll need to pay special attention to ensuring the drug goes into a container that's suitable for its particular characteristics. Also, there should be instructions on the label for beyond-use dates. The label needs to clearly state the medication's expiration date, whether the medication is aqueous or non-aqueous, what temperature to store it at, and it needs to include references to information on the medications' stability as well as the *United States Pharmocopeia* (USP) *27,* which contains most of the FDA's guidelines for compounding.

5. *Selecting Ingredients.* There are a lot of different places that ingredients can come from, but best practices state you should try to order chemicals from the USP or the National Formulary (NF.) That's because chemicals from these sources are guaranteed to be pure and safe. There are other chemical suppliers, but your pharmacist is responsible for making sure they meet all regulations and standards for making pharmaceuticals from those drugs. If necessary, you can use ingredients extracted from other manufactured medications that have been deemed acceptable by the FDA.

6. *Compounded preparations.* Unless there are laws in place that demand stricter accuracy, compounded preparations should be at least 90% and no more than 110% of the labeled active ingredient.

7. *The process of compounding.* According to the USP, the point of the compounding process is "to minimize errors and maximize the prescriber's intent." When you're in the process of compounding, keep the following in mind:
   - *The appropriateness of the prescription or medication order*
   - *Calculations of how much of each ingredient you need to use*
   - *The equipment needed to compound the drug*
   - *Proper hygiene and attire*
   - *Evaluation of final compound for variations in weight, proper mixture, and drug consistency*
   - *Correct notations in the compounding log*
   - *Correct labeling of the final product*
   - *Correct cleaning and storage of all equipment after compounding is complete.*

8. *Records and documents required for compounding.* Pharmacies are legally required to keep something called a master formula, which is also known as a formulation record. They also need to maintain a compounding record to keep track of every compounded preparation made at the pharmacy. The reason pharmacies are required to keep these records is so that compounders can reference each other's formulations. There are two parts of the "records and documents" portion of the PTCB:
   - *Formula (or formulation record.)* This is a record kept of all compounded preparations made in the pharmacy. The files are not

dissimilar to recipes in a cookbook – they include ingredients, equipment needed and mixing instructions.

- *Batch log (or compounding record).* This is the record of the actual preparation of any batch. It includes the internal identification number (also called the lot number) of the chemicals used in the mix as well as the manufacturers' numbers. The compounding record also contains data on the date the compound was created, any beyond-use date (if applicable) and any other information the compounder thinks is necessary to have on file regarding this particular batch.

9. *Quality control.* This is the last chance you get as a compounder to make sure the mix of chemicals you've made is as safe and high-quality as possible. Proper quality control is done by checking and double-checking not only the physical properties of the mix, but also the specific procedures used to make it to ensure they did it right the first time. If the compounder finds any errors in their processes – not matter how minor – a pharmacist will have to check the final compound to determine whether or not it's still acceptable.

For more information about compounding, consult the *United States Pharmocopeia* (also known as USP 27,) specifically Chapter 795, which covers non-sterile prep, Chapter 797, which covers sterile prep, and Chapter 1075, which is titled "Good Compounding ractices."

Equipment for Compounding in a Non-Sterile Environment

If you don't use the best, most current specialized equipment for compounding, you run the risk of creating a medication that's of inferior quality, or impure. Here is a list of equipment you'll most commonly use when compounding in a non-sterile environment:

- *Electronic Balance.* This piece of equipment is used to measure chemicals in a quick, accurate manner.

- *Glass or plastic graduates.* These are cylinders and conicals used to measure liquid volume. You should always use the smallest graduate possible when measuring liquids, and ensure that the graduate is on a flat, stable surface. When measuring with a graduate, ensure that you read from the bottom of the meniscus.

- *Pill tile.* Also known as an ointment slab, this is a square tile made of glass used to make creams, topical solutions and ointments. Some pharmacies prefer to use ointment paper, which is usually a square-foot stretch of parchment paper, because it's easier to clean up after compounding.

- *Mortar and pestle.* This is one of the most instantly recognizable pieces of equipment in the pharmacist's array. The mortar is a cylindrical bowl, usually made of glass, Wedgwood, ceramic or porcelain. The pestle is a bludgeon used to pound ingredients into the mortar's well. When mixing with a mortar and pestle, move the pestle in a circular motion. The process of reducing a large material to minute particles or fragments is called comminution. Reducing the particle size of an already ground-up compound is called triturated.

- *Ointment mill.* This is a mill, as the name suggests, with three rollers and adjustable spaces, used to reduce the particle size of a particular compound. Most compounding pharmacies have one of these in inventory.

Overview of Intravenous Medicine

Medications are typically administered to patients orally. When a drug needs to be administered in another way, such as through IV, nasally or otherwise, it's called *parenteral* administration.

The most common type of parenteral administration is intravenous, also known as IV. IV solutions are usually used to rehydrate patients or to quickly introduce drugs into their blood streams. Delivering a drug through IV can have many benefits that orally administered medication doesn't; for instance, a patient who is unconscious, nauseous or belligerent can be administered medication through IV.

However, it also has its disadvantages:

- It's painful for patients
- It carries a small risk of infection, if non-sterile equipment or solutions are used. The most common way by which equipment or solutions become non-sterile is through an administrator's touch between the pharmacy and the site of administration.
- If a pharmacist or administrator has made a mistake, or the patient is allergic, the rapid effects of intravenous administration can be difficult to counteract.
- It has a unique disadvantage, in that it may cause a condition called air embolus. This is when an injection creates an air bubble in the patient's vein, which can be harmful or even fatal. If an adult rapidly gets between 150-200 ml of air in their bloodstream, they can be damaged. These days, most IV solutions are performed with a gravity feed or an infusion pump that helps to prevent this from happening.
- IV can also cause something called extravasation. This happens when a catheter goes straight through a vein, rather than into it; this can happen when it's being inserted, or after it's already in the patient's vein, if the patient moves around too much. This can be painful for the patient, and

depending on the drug, it can be severely harmful – for instance, some chemotherapy can destroy muscle and tissue so thoroughly in the case of extravasation that a patient may end up needing surgery or amputation.

- Lastly, IV can cause phlebitis. This is an irritation or swelling of the vein. There are a lot of reasons this might happen, but the most common are because the drug itself is agitating, or the administration of the medication is happening quickly. Sometimes, it's because of particulates (particles of something other than the intended medication in the solution) or pyrogens (bacteria present on the needle or in the solution.) Phlebitis usually causes intense pain for a patient, usually along the path of the vein, and can sometimes cause the vein to swell up and turn red, and become visible under the skin.

If you want to be able to prepare and deliver IV medication, you'll need a specialized skill set and training in something called aseptic technique, which is also used in other parenteral administrations, like opthalmics.

Preparing a Saline or Dextrose Solution

Two of the most common IV drips you'll prepare working in a hospital pharmacy are saline and dextrose. Use the following table to help you study how to prepare the most common configurations of these solutions.

Solution	Abbreviation	Also Written As	Contents
Normal Saline	NS	0.9% NaCl (sodium chloride)	0.9g NaCl in 100 mL of water
Half Normal Saline	½NS	0.45% NaCl	0.45g NaCl in 100 mL of water
Quarter Normal Saline	¼NS	0.225% NaCl	0.225 g NaCl in 100 mL of water
Dextrose 5% In Water	D5W	5% Dextrose in Water	5g Dextrose in 100 mL of water
Dextrose 10% in Water	D10W	10% Dextrose in Water	10g Dextrose in 100 mL of water
Dextrose 5% in Normal Saline	D5NS	5% Dextrose in 0.9% NaCl	5g Dextrose and 0.9g NaCl in 100 mL of water

Aseptic Technique and Aseptic Preparation of Medications and Solutions

The aseptic preparation of IV solutions and other parenteral drugs in a sterile environment is a complicated, but necessary program in many pharmacies. Here are the main points:

1. *Always use proper aseptic technique when preparing or administering sterile medications and solutions.* Proper aseptic technique means always using a sterile, aseptic work environment, following strict aseptic guidelines and using sterile equipment.

2. A sterile, aseptic environment involves cleaning the counters, floors and any working surfaces daily. The walls, ceilings and any shelves used for storage should be cleaned at least on a monthly basis, but it's better to do it every two weeks. A sterile environment is also separate from any other

area in the pharmacy to avoid the introduction of fine particles into any solutions being prepared, foot traffic in and out is minimized, trash cans are emptied outside the room, and no cardboard is allowed. Some hospitals and pharmacies have aseptic compounding rooms with highly sensitive air filtration systems, ultraviolet radiation, positive room air pressure and more to reduce the particulate load that could potentially contaminate an aseptic solution.

3. A sterile, aseptic environment also involves the use of a horizontal or vertical laminar airflow workbench (called an LAFW), which filters air in the work area. Many people know the LAFW as a HEPA filter, although a HEPA filter is only one part of an LAFW. HEPA stands for High-Efficiency Particulate Air.

4. When using any LAFW, the most important thing to remember is that the flow of air between the HEPA filter and the sterile work space needs to remain uninterrupted. This is called the critical area.

5. Horizontal LAFWs move filtered air from the back of the hood to the front with a blower, while pulling contaminated air through a filter. With horizontal LAFWs, the critical area is behind the sterile object.

6. Vertical LAFWs are used during the preparation of some drugs that may be harmful to the health of the compounder. They move HEPA down into a work space and pull it back up into the ceiling. With vertical LAFWs, the critical area is above a sterile object.

7. All work done with an LAFW must be performed six inches from the sides and the front of the hood without obstructing any of the air vents.

8. LAFWs should always be:
   - Placed so they're in the area of the room with the lowest foot traffic
   - Run for 15-30 minutes before use
   - Cleaned with 70% isopropyl alcohol before using (although nothing can come in contact with the HEPA filter – not even cleaning solution)
   - Tested every six months or whenever the LAFW is moved.

9. Strict aseptic guidelines include:
   - Wearing appropriate clothing and attire. In an aseptic, sterile environment, don't wear jewelry, and be sure you're wearing shoe covers, hair and facial hair covers and face masks. If your pharmacy provides a scrub suit, wear that – but don't let it out of the anteroom, or it could get too many particulates on it.
   - Washing hands vigorously and thoroughly. You've got to wash your hands and arms up to your elbows for 30 seconds with a brush, proper soap and warm water before handling aseptic products.
   - Wear antiseptic, sterile gloves that have not left the work area.

10. Using proper sterile equipment means using:
   - Sterile plastic or glass syringes and needles from .5 to 60 ml
   - Sterile needles
   - Sterile vials and ampules

Syringes, Needles, Vials, Ampules and Automatic Compounders

These are pieces of equipment used in non-sterile, sterile and aseptic compounding, and you'll need to know a bit about them for the PTCB exam. Here's a quick primer:

Syringes

Syringes are a small device for holding chemical compounds that are made up of a barrel and a plunger. A needle can be affixed to the end of the syringe to administer IV medication. They range in what they can hold from .5 ml to 60 ml, and have calibration marks along the barrel that delineate volume.

You should always use the smallest syringe that you have available when compounding; syringes are designed to be filled between ½ and 2/3 capacity. This is because the smaller the syringe, the more accurate the calibration marks will help you to be. Syringes are accurate to a range of ½ the smallest calibration increment mark on the barrel.

Since most chemicals are more stable in glass than in plastic, pharmacies tend to use glass syringes more often when the medication is to be stored in the syringe for some time. You'll most often encounter plastic syringes in sterile environments where the medication won't be in contact with the syringe for an extended period of time.

Syringes are shipped sterile, so until you open the package, they're free of contamination. However, make sure and inspect the packaging of each syringe before you use it for compounding; if there's a tear in the plastic or any other breach of the packaging's integrity, you may have a non-sterile syringe on your hands. If you're working in an aseptic environment, always open the syringe within the purview of the laminar hood.

Needles

Needles are pretty simple contraptions, but they're actually made up of five components. The top of a needle is called the hub, and it's how you attach it to a syringe. The shaft is the metal that makes up the needle itself, and is usually lubricated with sterile silicone. The sharp tip of the needle is cut at an angle to form something called a bevel. The point of the bevel is called the bevel tip and the bottom of the bevel is called the bevel heel.

Needles have many different sizes, but they're measured two ways: The length of the needle, and the width (which is called the gauge.)

The length of a needle is measured in inches; the smallest needles available are usually 3/8 of an inch, and the largest go up to 3 ½ inches.

The gauge is a little bit counterintuitive – it's inversely correspondent to the diameter of the inside of the shaft of the needle, so the larger the gauge, the smaller the needle. The smallest possible gauge on a needle is 27, and the largest is 13.

Like syringes, needles are shipped sterile from the manufacturer, so inspect their packaging before opening it to make sure it's intact, and take all precautions in an aseptic environment to maintain their sterility.

Vials and Ampules

Vials are containers usually made of glass (for the same reason that syringes are.) Vials have a rubber stopper or flip-top cap at the top, and are used to hold both powders and liquids. Many vials are designed to be penetrated by a needle.

Vials are closed-system containers, meaning that gases (like air) and liquids (like moisture or the chemical itself) can't pass through them freely. Because air can't pass through a vial, sometimes there are differences in air pressure between that in the room and that in thevial. To prevent a vacuum from forming inside the vial, you'll need to inject as much air into the vial as the amount of liquid you're planning to withdraw. Of course, you don't want to do this if the drug you're working with produces gas, such as cytotoxic chemicals.

Ampules are glass, and unlike vials, are closed-system containers only until they're opened. This neatly solves the air pressure problem with vials, but it also means that once an ampule is open, the sterility of a chemical could potentially be compromised if the ampule is opened outside of an aseptic environment. Before breaking an ampule, always clean it well with an alcohol swab and leave it in place when you're finished.

Automatic Compounders

Because sterile compounding isn't easy, and requires such meticulous attention to detail and patience, a lot of hospitals have installed automatic compounders in their sterile areas to reduce the likelihood of human error. You'll need specialized training to operate these depending on the kind of equipment used and which manufacturer makes it.

Labeling IV Solutions

Once you've finished compounding a sterile product, you need to label it. Most pharmacies have implemented a system involving bar codes to prevent mistakes from being made, and this will probably be the case where you work. However, if that system goes down, you have to know how to properly label an IV solution!

There are 11 elements to a proper label:

1. The name of the patient, their identification number, and the number of the room they're in, if necessary.
2. The sequence number of the bag or bottle, if necessary
3. The name of the drug and the amount in the container

4. The name of the admixture solution, and the volume

5. The final total volume of the admixture, if necessary

6. The prescribed flow rate (ml/hour)

7. The date and time the drug is scheduled to be administered to the patient

8. The date and time the drug was prepared

9. The expiration date

10. The initials of the person who prepared the solution, and the initials of the person who checked it

11. Any ancillary instructions or warnings that health care workers need to know before administering the medication

Preparing and Handling Hazardous Medications

Many drugs, including cytotoxic medications and drugs used for chemotherapy, are potentially hazardous to people that touch, inhale or ingest them. They're only supposed to be used, after all, when it's a life or death situation! For a pharmacy technician, these drugs can be dangerous, so it's important to know how to handle them.

Any time you're handling a potentially hazardous drug, you'll need to wear protective equipment, personal protective equipment such as gloves, goggles and a mask, and follow specific procedures for handling spills or disposing of waste.

Hazardous drugs will most often be stored in a vertical LAFW called a Biological Safety Cabinet, which will help them maintain the highest level of sterility possible and protect the people who are working with and around them. Biological Safety Cabinets need to be on 24 hours per day and seven days per week, and should be inspected and certified every six months. Horizontal LAFWs are not a legal or safe alternative to Biological Safety Cabinets.

Your pharmacy will have specific guidelines for technicians that work with hazardous and cytotoxic medications, so you'll have to complete a special training course before you begin working with them.

Chapter 2: Mathematics, Calculations and Units of Measure

This part is technically listed under the "Assisting the Pharmacist in Serving Patients" portion of the PTCB exam, but it's such a large part of the test (and the part that scares people so badly) that this book is devoting an entire chapter to it.

Here's all of the information you'll need to be able to pass this portion of the test.

Arabic and Roman Numerals

Arabic Numerals

Arabic numerals are the ones you learned as a toddler: 0, 1, 2, 3, 4, 5, 6, 7, 8 and 9. Arabic numerals have steadily replaced Roman numerals as the numbers of choice for pharmacy notation.

Roman Numerals

Roman numerals use letters to represent numbers. You may have learned this in school, but most people aren't very familiar with this system. Especially in the case of controlled substances, when prescribers are writing quantities for dispensation or units of medication they want the patient to take, they will often use Roman numerals because the numerals are more difficult for unscrupulous patients to change.

Here's a table with the Roman numerals:

ss = ½	I = 1	V = 5
X = 10	L = 50	C = 100
M = 1000		

There are three rules you need to remember regarding Roman numerals:

1. *If a numeral of **equal/lesser** value comes **after** a numeral of **equal/greater** value, **add** the numerals.* For instance, to write the number 6 in Roman numerals, you would write VI, because V (5) + I (1) = VI (6). To write the number 15, you would write XV. To write the letter 160, you would write CLX.

2. *Never repeat a numeral more than three times.*

3. *If a numeral of **lesser value** is placed **before** a numeral of **greater value**, you need to **subtract** the numeral of **lesser value**.* For instance, to write the number 4 in roman numerals, you would write IV, because I (1) is less than V(5) so it's 5-1 = 4. The reason for this is that a numeral can't be repeated more than three times. The number III (3) already has the number I (1) repeated three times, so 4 must be IV. Using this rule, to write the number 29, one would write XXIX.

On the PTCB exam, you'll be asked to perform <u>addition</u>, <u>subtraction</u>, <u>multiplication</u> and <u>division</u> and some other basic math regarding fractions. Let's get down to some definitions, first.

Numerators and Denominators

In a fraction, the number on top of the line is called a <u>numerator</u>. The number on the bottom of the line is called a <u>denominator</u>.

Mixed Numbers

Mixed numbers are a combination of whole numbers and fractions.

Common Denominator

A common denominator means that the denominator in two or more fractions in the same equation are equal to each other. When we talk about the "lowest common denominator," we're referring to the furthest point that two fractions can be reduced so that they can be added, subtracted, etc. It's not possible to add or subtract fractions if they haven't been reduced to a common denominator. In order to find the lowest common denominator, you multiply the numerator and the denominator of both fractions by the denominator of the other.

Reducing Fractions

In order to reduce a fraction, you'll divide both the numerator and the denominator by the lowest common divisor (LCD). The LCD is the lowest number that both the numerator and denominator can divide into and still be a whole number.

For instance, $\frac{6}{8}$ is equal to $\frac{3}{4}$. Both 6 and 8 are divisible by 2, which is the LCD. 6 divided by 2 equals 3, and 8 divided by 2 equals 4.

We can't reduce $\frac{3}{4}$ any further, because 3 and 4 do not have a LCD that produces a whole number.

If your numerator is larger than your denominator, you'll need to reduce the fraction to a mixed number. For example: $\frac{15}{6}$ has an LCD of 3. 15 divided by 3 becomes 5, and 6 divided by 3 equals . Thus, $\frac{15}{6}$ becomes $\frac{5}{2}$. $\frac{5}{2}$ becomes $2\frac{1}{2}$.

Addition

There are three very simple steps to follow when adding fractions:

1. Make sure the denominators are the same by using the lowest common denominator method.
2. Add the numerators and put the value over the (now common) denominator.
3. Reduce the fraction (if necessary.)

Here's an example:

$$\frac{1}{3} + \frac{1}{6} = ?$$

We can't add these fractions until we get the denominators lined up. In order to do this, we'll have to convert both fractions into a common denominator. We'll do this by converting the smallest denominator into the largest.

We know that the number "6" is twice as big as the number 3, right? After all 3 x 2 =6.

$$\frac{1*2}{3*2} = \frac{2}{6}$$

So now we add the numerators, and our equation becomes:

$$\frac{2}{6} + \frac{1}{6} = \frac{3}{6}$$

The last step is to reduce the fraction. What is the lowest number we can find that both 3 and 6 can divide into while producing a whole number?

The answer is…3! 3 divided by 3 equals 1, and 6 divided by 3 equals 2. Thus, we reduce the fraction like this:

$$\frac{3/3}{6/3} = \frac{1}{2}$$

And now we have the answer to our problem:

$$\frac{1}{3} + \frac{1}{6} = \frac{1}{2}$$

Subtraction

Just as with adding fractions, there are three simple rules to follow when subtracting them:

1. Make sure the denominators are the same by using the lowest common denominator method.
2. Subtract the numerators and put the value over the (now common) denominator.
3. Reduce the fraction (if necessary.)

It works just like addition, only you subtract the numerators rather than adding them. Pretty simple!

Here's an example:

$$\frac{1}{2} - \frac{1}{3} = ?$$

Since the denominators are different, we have to find the lowest number that both 2 and 3 can *factor* into, rather than *divide* into. In this case, we know that 2 x 3 =6. Thus, "6" is our common denominator, and we have to convert both fractions.

$$\frac{1*3}{2*3} = \frac{3}{6}$$

$$\frac{1*2}{3*2} = \frac{2}{6}$$

So now we place the fraction side by side and subtract the numerators, and our equation becomes:

$$\frac{3}{6} - \frac{2}{6} = \frac{1}{6}$$

The last step is to reduce the fraction. But in this case, there's no need to do so.

Multiplication

When multiplying fractions, you don't have to find the lowest common denominators – so it's much easier! You simply multiply straight across (numerators to numerators, denominators to denominators) and then reduce the fraction.

Here's an example:

$$\frac{4}{5} \times \frac{3}{8} = \frac{12}{40}$$ because 4 x 3 = 12, and 5 x 8 = 40.

Now, we just reduce that fraction by dividing both the numerator and denominator by 2 until we can't get whole numbers anymore.

$$\frac{12}{40} \text{ becomes } \frac{6}{20} \text{ becomes } \frac{3}{10}$$

Voila! The answer is 3/10.

Division

Dividing fractions, like multiplying, is pretty simple, since you don't have to find the lowest common denominator. Instead, you use the *inversion trick.*

The inversion trick is simple. To divide fractions, you actually *multiply* the first fraction by the inverse of the second fraction.

Here's an example.

$$\frac{4}{5} \div \frac{3}{8} = ?$$

Simply invert the second fraction, and change the division sign to a multiplication sign.

$$\frac{4}{5} \times \frac{8}{3} = \frac{32}{15}$$

Now, 32 and 15 don't have a lowest common divisor, but we can reduce this fraction by turning it into a mixed number. 15 goes into 32 twice, with two left over. Thus, the answer to the original problem is:

$$\frac{4}{5} \div \frac{3}{8} = 2\frac{2}{15}$$

Working With Decimal Numbers

On the PTCB, you'll be asked to perform a lot of calculations with decimal numbers, including conversions of mixed numbers and fractions.

It's *extremely important* that you check and double check all calculations you make regarding decimals. If you do the math wrong, or write an illegible equation, you could be setting someone up for a misinterpretation that could lead to a major dosing error. A patient's health is depending on your penmanship and skill with math!

Here are two ground rules for using decimals:

1. *Only use decimals when necessary.* Outside of one specific occasion (which we'll cover later) you should never write a whole number as a decimal. For instance, if you need 4 of something, you should always write 4, not 4.0. The decimal point and zero – which in this case is called a <u>trailing</u> zero - re never necessary – and could lead someone to misinterpret your number as 40 instead of 4!

2. *Strongly demarcate your decimal points.* When you're performing calculations by hand, and planning to give it to someone else to look at, it's very important to clearly demarcate your decimal points. Make them big and dark, so that no one has a chance to misinterpret the fact that you're using a decimal number.

3. *Never write a decimal point unless there's a number in front of it.* If you need .75 of something, you need to express it as 0.75. There should always be a zero on the front of a partial number rendered as a decimal number. This is called a <u>leading</u> zero. You wouldn't want someone to accidentally use 75 ml of a drug instead of .75!

Now that you've got the rules, here are the basic functions you need to know when working with decimals:

Converting Fractions to Decimals

This is nice and simple: You just divide the numerator by the denominator.

$$\frac{4}{5} \text{ becomes } 4 \div 5$$

4 divided by 5 = 0.8

Converting Mixed Numbers to Decimals

This also pretty easy. But there are two steps in the process of converting mixed numbers to decimals:

1. Convert the mixed number to a fraction. This is the opposite process of reducing a fraction. Essentially, you multiply the denominator of the fraction by the whole number and add it to the numerator. Here's what it looks like:

$$2\frac{2}{15} \text{ becomes } \frac{32}{15}$$

2. Now, you have a fraction, so you follow the formula for converting fractions to decimals. Simply divide the numerator by the denominator.

$$\frac{32}{15} \text{ becomes } 32 \div 15$$

32 divided by 15 = 2.13

Converting Decimals to Fractions or Mixed Numbers

Once again, we have a two-step process. Let's start with a simple number: 2.2

1. Make a fraction by turning the decimal number into the numerator and setting the denominator as 1.0.

$$\frac{2.2}{1.0}$$

2. Move the decimal point over on both the numerator and denominator an equal number of spaces until there are no more integers on the numerator.

$$\frac{2.2}{1.0} \text{ becomes } \frac{22.0}{10.0}$$

We know that we can strike the .0 from the end of both of these fractions now. That means we have a fraction!

$$\frac{22}{10}$$

We can further reduce this to:

$$\frac{11}{5}$$

And now we have our answer.

Working with Percentages

Percentages are fractions with an unchanging denominator, rendered as decimals.

The denominator is always 100. This makes it nice and easy to do conversions.

Converting Percentages to Fractions

Simply write the percentage number as the numerator over a denominator of 100, then reduce the fraction. For instance, let's say we want to make 75% into a fraction.

$$75\% \text{ becomes } \frac{75}{100}$$

Now, we reduce the fraction. The lowest common divisor of both of these numbers is 25.

$$\frac{75 \div 25}{100 \div 25} = \frac{3}{4}$$

3/4 is our answer.

Converting Fractions to Percentages

This is a four-step process. Let's walk through it using 5/8 as an example.

1. Convert the fraction into decimals.

$$\frac{5}{8} \text{ becomes } 5 \div 8$$

5 divided by 8 = 0.625.

2. Now, place the decimal over a denominator of 1, with trailing zeros to the end of the numerators decimal place.

$$\frac{0.625}{1.000}$$

3. Now, move the decimal point over on both the numerator and denominator an equal number of spaces until the denominator equals 100.

$$\frac{0.625}{1.000} \text{ becomes } \frac{62.5}{100} \text{ becomes } 62.5\%$$

And we have our answer: 5/8 is equal to 62.5 percent.

Working With Ratios and Proportions

First, here are some definitions: A ratio shows the relationship between two numbers. For instance, a patient may need to take a certain amount of a medication depending on their weight. If they need to take 10 milligrams for every 10 kilograms that they weigh, then the ratio is 10mg/10kg. This is also sometimes written as 10mg:10kg, although the slash (/) is more common than the colon (:)

If two ratios use the same units, you can combine them to create a proportion.

You need to have a thorough mastery of ratios and proportions, especially when compounding and preparing medications. In fact, most of your pharmacy calculations (and many of the calculations you have to perform on the PTCB exam) involve ratios and proportions. Most of the time, when it comes to medications, the ratio is usually how many grams (the weight) of a drug (here called the solute) goes into how many milliliters of a solution.

It can seem complicated at first, but the process of calculating ratios and proportions is actually quite simple.

If the ratio of solute to solution is 1 mg to 2 mL, you have a ratio of 1/2. You can also read this as a fraction: The 1 is the numerator, and the 2 is the denominator.

If you recall, a proportion is just a statement that says two ratios are equal to each other. Finding the proportion is necessary for determining how much solute to put in a solution.

For instance, you may need to mix a cough syrup that has a ratio of 5 mg/10 mL, but the prescription calls for 100 mL. You need to calculate the new ratio to make sure there's the proper amount of solute in 100 mL of solution. Here's what the equation looks like:

$$\frac{5 \text{ mg}}{10 \text{ mL}} = \frac{???}{100 \text{ mL}}$$

So in order to find the proportion, we need to determine the difference between the ratio and the number on the prescription. In this case, we can simply divide 100 mL by 10 mL and receive the number 10, which is known in mathematics as the <u>means</u>. Now, we multiply 5 mg by the means, which is 10, and we get 50 mg. So we know the cough syrup needs to have 50 mg of solute in 100 mL of solution.

Here's another way of expressing it that you may encounter in a real-world situation:

A is to *B* as *Y* is to *Z*.

If you hear someone say this, they're verbally representing this equation:

$$\frac{A}{B} = \frac{Y}{Z}$$

If you look at the above equation, you'll realize it's identical to the previous example – again, all you have to do is find the means, and you can work out ratios and proportions.

Units of Measure

These can be somewhat confusing, because in the United States, we use several different units of measure simultaneously, and it's your job to make the conversions between them.

Let's get into the details of each measuring system you'll encounter. You probably already have varying levels of familiarity with each of these.

The Household System

If you've done any cooking or baking, you know this system pretty well. And having that familiarity is useful, because the household system is the most widely used in retail pharmacies. This system involves teaspoons and tablespoons, and it's common practice to give out a properly measured spoon along with a dispensed prescription to make sure patients can accurately measure their own doses.

One part of the household system still in common use is the measurement called "drop." Be careful with this! The consistency of a liquid can affect how big or small a drop is, and so can the size and shape of the dropper. It's better to use a milliliter dropper, which accurately measures 1 mL per drop, than to leave it up to the patient. The exception to this is in the case of eye drops, which come with a dropper designed to dispense the right amount of solution.

The Avoirdupois System

This is one of the older systems still in use, but you'll recognize it immediately: It's based on the pound, which is made up of 16 ounces. The name of the system comes from the French *avoir de pois*, which means "goods of weight."

The Metric System

This is the most accurate measuring system in wide use today, and should act as your default. Most Americans aren't terribly familiar with the metric system because we still use the Royal System developed in England (inches, feet, miles, etc.) However, the metric system has clear advantages over every other measuring system.

The standard measures in the metric system are the meter (for length,) the gram (for weight) and the liter (for volume.) The values of these measures vary depending on their prefix. The tables below have the common prefixes used in the metric system.

Prefixes for Length (Meters)	Notes
Kilo	This means 1000. 1000 meters is a kilometer (km.)
Cent	This means 1/100. 1/100 meters is a centimeter (cm.)
Mil	This means 1/1000. 1/1000 meters is a millimeter (mm.)

Prefixes for Weight (Grams)	Notes
Kilo	This means 1000. 1000 grams is a kilogram (kg.)
Mil	This means 1/1000. 1/1000 grams is a milligram (mg.)
Micro	This means 1 millionth. 1/1,000,000 of a gram is a microgram (mcg.)

Prefixes for Volume (Liters)	Notes
Deci	This means 1/10. 1/10 of a liter is a deciliter (dL.)
Mil	This means 1/1000. 1/1000 liters is a milliliter (mL.)
Micro	This means 1 millionth. 1/1,000,000 of a liter is a microliter (mcL.)

Converting the Metric System to Other Systems

There isn't a good, one-to-one relationship between these different systems of measurement, so it's best to default to the metric system. However, as a pharmacy technician, you'll be called on to make conversions on a regular basis. Use the tables below for weights and measures.

Length – Metric System to Household System

Metric	Household
2.54 centimeters	1 inch

Volume – Metric System to Household System

Metric	Household
5 milliliters	1 teaspoon
15 milliliters	1 tablespoon
30 milliliters	1 fluid ounce

473 milliliters	1 pint

Volume – Within the Household System

Household	Household
1 cup	8 fluid ounces
2 cups	1 pint
2 pints	1 quart
4 quarts	1 gallon

Mass – Metric System to Avoirdupois System

Metric	Avoirdupois
1 kilogram	2.2 pounds
454 grams	1 pound
28.4 grams	1 ounce

Converting Household to Metric

The ratio and proportion method we learned earlier (A is to B as X is to Y) can help you convert household to metric units. Simply set up your units of measurement (for example, milliliters and teaspoons) in the same fashion as you set up solutes and solutions previously, then find the means and take it from there.

Temperature – Celsius and Fahrenheit

Around the world, the most commonly used system for measuring temperature is called Celsius. In America, Belize and Jamaica, we use the Fahrenheit system. Fahrenheit is a slightly more accurate system of measuring temperature in whole degrees, but using decimals, Celsius is a perfectly fine system for pharmacology.

Converting Fahrenheit to Celsius

You won't often work with Celsius temperatures, but you have to know how this conversion for the PTCB exam, so here goes. To convert Fahrenheit to Celsius, follow these steps.

1. Measure the temperature in Fahrenheit.
2. Subtract 32 degrees.
3. Multiply the remainder by 5/9.

For example, let's convert 70 degrees Fahrenheit to Celsius. We'll subtract 32 degrees, giving us 38. Then, we multiply 38 by 5/9 (which, if you do your decimal conversion, is about 0.56,) giving us a temperature of about 21 degrees Celsius (rounded down.)

Converting Celsius to Fahrenheit

This is a similar process, with a couple of twists. Follow these steps to convert Celsius to Fahrenheit:

1. Measure the temperature in Celsius.
2. Multiply the temperature by 9/5.
3. Add 32 degrees.

For example, let's convert those 21 degrees Celsius back to Fahrenheit. First, we'll multiply 21 by 9/5 (which is 1.8) for a value of 37.8. 37.8 + 32 = 69.8; if you round that up, we're back to 70 degrees Fahrenheit!

Converting Time – Modular to Military Time

Most hospitals and medical institutions use the 24 hour system (also known as military time) rather than the 12 hour system (also known as modular time) when writing instructions for the administration of medication. The 24 hour system does not have AM or PM – rather, it counts the hours and minutes since midnight. It goes from 0 – 23, and has no colon like the 12 hour system.

It takes a little time to get used to this – even soldiers screw it up once in a while, because of the prevalence of the 12 hour system in our society – but once you've got it, you'll never forget it. Here's a chart:

12 Hour System (Modular Time)	24 Hour System (Military Time)
0000 (Midnight)	12:00 AM
0100	1:00 AM
0200	2:00 AM
0300	3:00 AM
0400	4:00 AM
0500	5:00 AM
0600	6:00 AM
0700	7:00 AM

0800	8:00 AM
0900	9:00 AM
1000	10:00 AM
1100	11:00 AM
1200	12:00 PM
1300	1:00 PM
1400	2:00 PM
1500	3:00 PM
1600	4:00 PM
1700	5:00 PM
1800	6:00 PM
1900	7:00 PM
2000	8:00 PM
2100	9:00 PM
2200	10:00 PM
2300	11:00 PM

Minutes work exactly the way you would expect them to – if it's 3:30 AM in 12 hour time, it's 0330 in 24 hour time. If it's 5:15 in 12 hour time, it's 1715 in 24 hour time. You get the drift.

Body Surface Area

Despite our earlier example, basing dosage information for certain drugs off of a patient's weight is not actually the best and most accurate method for determining how much of a medication a patient should receive. The most common method for this called body surface area, and it takes into account both a patient's weight and their height.

You'll most commonly encounter calculations for body surface area when handling chemotherapy drugs. It's always expressed in the metric system – never the royal system, which uses inches and feet.

The body surface area equation is, by far, the most complicated formula we've seen to date. But have no fear! In the real world, the computer will do this for you. However, this equation sometimes shows up on the PTCB exam – after all, you'll need to know this if the computers ever go down – so we'll go through it step-by-step. Here's the formula, also known as the Mosteller formula:

$$BSA(m^2) = \sqrt{\frac{[\text{height (cm)} * \text{weight (kg)}]}{3600}}$$

To perform this equation, follow these steps:

1. First, plug in the patient's height in centimeters and weight in kilograms. Let's say we have a 150 lb. male who is 5'10". His weight in kilograms is 68.2, and his height in centimeter is 177.8 cm.

$$BSA(m^2) = \sqrt{\frac{177.8 * 68.2}{3600}} \text{ becomes } BSA(m^2) = \sqrt{\frac{12125.96}{3600}}$$

2. Now, we reduce that fraction and get its principle square root (that's what that symbol that looks like a check mark and a ceiling over the fraction is.)

$$\text{BSA}(m^2) = \sqrt{3.3683} \text{ becomes } \text{BSA}(m^2) = 1.8352929$$

And we have our answer. The patient's BSA is 1.8352929.

Dosage Calculations

Here are the basics: When you're calculating a dose, you need three pieces of information:

1. The number of doses
2. The total amount of the drug
3. The size of a dose

The reason you need all three is because if you have any two of these, you can find the third. Here's how they all work together: The number of doses is always equal to the total amount of the drug divided by the size of the prescribed dose. If you want the equation, try it this way:

Total amount of drug = (number of doses) x (size of dose).

How to Calculate a Dose Based on a Patient's Weight

Some medications, like chemotherapy or medications for children, are based on a patient's weight. Usually, they're prescribed at 1 unit per 1 kilogram of the patient's body weight.

Remembering that kilograms are 2.2 pounds, you'll have to use your experience with ratios and proportions to determine dose. Let's see an example.

If a doctor writes a prescription for 5 mg/1 kg per day, and the patient weighs 150 lbs., how many mg of medication do they need daily?

1. Calculate their weight in kilograms. A 150 lb. person weighs about 68.2 kg.

2. Multiply the dosage (5 mg) by their weight in kilograms (68.2).

3. We have our answer! 5 times 68.2 is about 341 kg.

So we know the patient needs to take 341kg of medication a day. But what if the doctor prescribes that the drug be taken three times a day? What size of doses need to be used?

Remember that as long as we have two out of three pieces of information – the number of doses, the total amount of the drug and the size of the dose, we can calculate dosage. In this case, we have the number of doses and the total amount of the drug that needs to be take daily.

Total amount of drug: 341 kg.

Number of doses: 3

Size of dose: ?

In this case, we simply divide the daily total amount of the drug by the daily number of doses to get the size of the dose. 341 kg divided by 3 gives us our answer as to what the size of each dose should be: about 114 mg.

How to Calculate Supply

Most medications need to be taken over a period of time in order to be effective. This means that you, as the pharmacy technician, will need to know how to ensure a patient gets an adequate supply of medication.

Calculating medication designed to be taken orally is quite simple. You simply multiply the number of doses per day by the number of days the medication is prescribed to be taken.

However, calculating a topical product is significantly more complicated.

Let's say a patient needs eye drops, and the doctor has written them a prescription for 2 drops in each eye twice a day for ten days. The bottle that will hold the drops is 5 milliliters, which is fairly standard, and 1 milliliter is equal to 20 drops for this particular solution (this is also very common.)

The prescription gives us two pieces of information:

1. The patient needs to take 4 drops, twice a day.
2. The patient needs to take these drops for 10 days.

How much solution does the patient need in order to have enough medication to complete their treatment?

Let's reason through it together:

1. 4 drops twice per day is 8 drops per day.
2. The length of treatment is 10 days.
3. Thus, the patient needs 80 drops.
4. 1 milliliter is equal to 20 drops.
5. Thus, the patient needs 4 milliliters of solution in order to have enough drops to finish treatment. (4*20 = 80 drops)

One note: It is okay, for prescriptions calling for medicines that are not on a controlled schedule, to be *overfilled* by a little bit. After all, we are human beings, and human beings make mistakes. What if the patient has a hard time with the eyedropper and misses his or her eye during application? You wouldn't want them to have to skip a dose and potentially not be healed of their affliction.

Overfilling a prescription is up to the discretion of the pharmacist, and again, depends on the type of medication, but as a technician, use your best judgment when filling a prescription, and if you think overfilling a prescription would be beneficial to a patient – and if it's wise, safe and legal, bring it up to the pharmacist.

Concentrating and Diluting

When a pharmacy mixture is created by mixing two liquids, you have to measure the strength of the drug in volume, which means using the metric system. Typically, the ratio you'll use is x mL/100 mL.

When you're mixing two solids together, you'll measure the strength of the medication by weight. Typically, the ratio will be x g/100 g

When you're mixing a solid and a liquid, you'll measure the strength by weight/volume. That is, how many grams (or milligrams) per liter (or milliliter?) Typically, it will be x mg/100 mL.

Expressing Concentration as a Percentage

We're back to ratios and proportions again. Concentrations as a percentage are essentially the same as material we've already covered. You'll work with three kinds of concentrations:

1. Weight-in-weight. This is the grams of drug per 100 grams of product.
2. Volume-in-volume. This is the liters of drug per 100 liters of product.
3. Weight-in-volume. This is the grams of drug per 100 liters of product.

We're back to A is to B as Y is to Z. In this case, you know the ratio of drugs to product, but when customizing a prescription, you'll have to solve for A to get the proportion correct.

Expressing Concentration as a Ratio Strength

Many solutions require only a very tiny amount of a drug in order to be effective. When this happens, you'll often see a ratio, as expressed with a slash (/) or colon (:).

For example, you may see that a particular solution is available in three concentrations: 1 mL/100 mL, 1 mL/1000 mL, and 1 mL/10,000 mL. You may also see them described as 1:100, 1:1000 and 1:10000.

Let's say a doctor orders 500 mL of a solution with a concentration of 1:1000. You know that 1,000 mL has 1 gram of medication in it, so how much medication should 500 mL have?

You know that 500 mL is one half of 1000 mL. So now you have the means: 0.5.

Multiply 1 gram by the means (0.5) and you get: 0.5.

So when mixing the solution, you know that you need 0.5 grams of drug for 500 mL of solution.

Calculating IV Flow Rates

If you're working in a hospital or in a home-care setting, you'll need to be able to perform calculations regarding IV flow rates.

All flow rates are measured in milliliters per hour, and are always whole numbers. Once again, you'll use a ratio and proportion method to calculate the flow rate. For example, if a patient would receive 500 mL of a solution in an hour (500 mL/1 hr) how many would they receive in a minute?

We know there are 60 minutes in an hour, so we have our means. Now, we divide 500 by 60, for a total of 8.3. Since all flow rates are whole numbers, we round down, and now we know our answer is 8.

Calculating Chemotherapy Dosages

If you're working in the oncology department of a hospital, it's critical that you understand how to properly administer very potent chemotherapy medications to your patients. If you don't do your calculations correct, you can cause a patient severe harm – or even death. Most places have systems of checks and redundancies to ensure that errors get caught before the medication goes out, but it's better to be right the first time, every time.

Once again, you'll use the ratio and proportions system here to get you through. It's all about finding the means and solving from there.

You receive a medication order for 200 mg/m^2 over 3 minutes, once daily. You know you need to prepare 200 mg of medication for every square meter of the patient's BSA. So you've got *A* and *B* right there.

As an example, let's say the patient is our 150 lb. man from before, who is also 5'10". We know that he has a BSA of 1.8352929 because we calculated it earlier using our formulation. In the pharmacy, you'll likely round the BSA to 1.84. Now, you've got a value for *Z*. You only have to solve for *Y*.

Knowing that you need 200 mg for every square meter of the patient's BSA, you multiply 200 by 1.84 for a total of 368 mg, and now you've got your answer for how much of the drug to prepare.

Statistics

This is a word that is dreaded by even most math majors, because statistics is unlike any other mathematical discipline, and requires a lot of skull sweat. There are some statistics problems that show up on the PTCB exam, but they are only regarding very simple concepts. Let's dive in:

The Arithmetic Mean

Do not confuse this with the means. This is a different concept! Finding an <u>arithmetic</u> <u>mean</u>, is all about finding the <u>average</u> of several sets of numbers. In order to find it, you divide the sum of a specific set of numbers by the total number of sets you've got.

Here's the formula:

$$A = \frac{1}{n} * \sum_{i=1}^{n} x_i$$

Where:

A = the average (or arithmetic mean)

N = the number of terms (that is, the total amount of sets of numbers you're averaging)

X_i = the value of each individual item in the list of numbers being averaged.

See? No problem! You're already a pro. On to the next section!

Okay, just kidding. We won't leave you out in the cold like that. This is a much easier way to represent it:

$$A = \frac{S}{N}$$

Where:

A = the average (or arithmetic means)

S = the sum of the numbers you want to average

N = the number of terms being averaged

To see this in action, let's say we want to find the arithmetic mean of these three numbers: 4, 6 and 8.

We can add these together to find S. $S = 18$.

Next, we know there are three different numbers we're averaging, so now we've got N. $N = 3$.

Since A is equal to S/N, and 18/3 is 6, we know that $A = 6$.

The Median

The median is a value in an ordered set of values; above and below it in its native set, there are an equal number of values. Essentially, if you have a long set of numbers, and you want to find the median, you're finding the middle.

To find the median, you have to find the arithmetic mean of the two values nearest to the middle of the set.

So let's apply this. Let's say you need to find the average age of ten pharmacy technicians. Here they are in a set.

24, 28, 31, 33, 35, 38, 38, 41, 42, 55

First, find the two values nearest to the middle of the set.

24, 28, 31, 33, **35, 38**, 38, 41, 42, 55

We've chosen 35 and 38 because there are four numbers to the left of 35, and four numbers to the left of 38.

Now, using the arithmetic means formula, we find their average.

35 + 38 = 73

73/2 = 36.5

And we have our answer. The average age of these ten pharmacy technicians is 36.5.

Calculating Specific Gravity

Take heart! This is the last part you need to study before you're finished with Mathematics and Calculations!

Every substance has a number unique to it called <u>specific gravity</u>. Specific gravity is defined as the ratio of the weight of the compound to the weight of the same amount of water. Basically, how heavy is a substance compared to water?

For instance, the specific gravity of ethanol is 0.787 – which means that ethanol is about 21% lighter than water. Ever wonder why people get the spins when they drink too much and try to lay down? It's because their blood is filled with ethanol (which is what alcohol metabolizes into,) which makes its specific gravity lighter than their body is used to.

When you're converting between weight and volume, it's useful to know a particular compound's specific gravity, although in a pharmacy setting, specific gravity and density are used interchangeably. Here's how to find the specific gravity of a substance:

$$specific\ gravity = \frac{weight\ (g)}{volume\ (mL)}$$

We know that 1 mL of water always weighs 1 gram, and vice-versa, because we know that the specific gravity of water is 1.

So if you need to find the weight of a particular liquid substance, you can use the ratio and proportion methods from earlier. Let's say you need to find the weight of a pint of milk. The specific gravity of milk is 1.035, and we know there are 473 mL in a pint.

We have three terms, so we need to find the means. There is 1.035 grams to every 1 milliliter in milk, so how many grams are in 473? 473 is the means, so we multiply 473 by 1.035 grams, and we have 489.55 – or about 490 grams for every pint of milk.

Chapter 3: List of Common Drugs

Below is an incomplete list of drugs you'll encounter on a day-to-day basis while working as a pharmacy technician. Some of these will appear on the PTCB, so it's important to have as many memorized as possible.

INOTROPIC AGENTS – commonly prescribed for congestive heart failure

Brand	Generic	Adverse Effects
Primacor	Milrinone	Thrombocytopenia (low platelet counts in blood)
Inocor	Amrinone	Ventricular arrhythmia (irregular movements of the heart's left ventricles
Lanoxin	Digoxin	Anorexia (appetite loss), Nausea

ANTIARRHYTHMIC AGENTS – commonly prescribed for irregular heart rhythm

Brand	Generic	Adverse Effects
Cerebyx	Phenytoin	Bleeding/inflamed gums, ataxia (inability to coordinate muscle movements)
Cordarone	Amiodarone	Pulmonary toxicity (lung toxicity)
Dilantin	Phenytoin	Bleeding/inflamed gums, ataxia
Ethmozine	Moricizine	A.V. node suppression (slowdown of the conduction velocity of the heart)

Norpace	Disopyramide	Dry eyes, blurred vision, negative inotropic effect (reduction of the force in a heartbeat)
Procanbid	Procainamide	S.L.E. (systemic lupus erythematosus, a chronic inflammatory disease of the connective tissues,) blood dyscrasia (a blood abnormality)
Quinidine	Quinidine	Diarrhea
Tambocor	Flecanide	A.V. node suppression
Tonocard	Tocainide	Pulmonary toxicity
Xylocaine	Lidocaine	CNS stimulation, seizure

BETA-BLOCKERS – commonly prescribed for hypertension and angina. Patients with Chronic Heart Failure, diabetes and asthma should not take beta-blockers.

Brand	Generic	Adverse Effects
Brevibloc	Esmolol	Bradycardia (slowing of the heart rate)
Coreg	Carvedilol	Bradycardia
Corgard	Nadolol	Bradycardia
Inderal	Propranolol	Bradycardia
Levatol	Penbutolol	Bradycardia
Lopressor	Metoprolol	Bradycardia
Normodyne	Labetalol	Bradycardia
Sectral	Acebutalol	Bradycardia

Tenormin	Atenolol	Bradycardia
Toprol XL	Metoprolol	Bradycardia
Trandate	Labetalol	Bradycardia
Zebeta	Bisoprolol	Bradycardia

CENTRALLY ACTING ANTIHYPERTENSIVE AGENTS – commonly prescribed for hypertension

Brand	Generic	Adverse Effects
Aldomet	Methldopa	Hemolytic anemia (lack of red blood cells)
Catepres	Clonidine	Hypotension (low blood pressure)
Tenex	Guanfacine	Hypotension
Wytensin	Guanabenx	Hypotension

CA-CHANNEL BLOCKERS – commonly prescribed for hypertension

Brand	Generic	Adverse Effects
Adalat	Nifedipine	Hypotension
Calan	Verapamil	Hypotension, constipation
Cardizem	Diltiazem	Hypotension
DynaCirc	Isradipine	Hypotension
Isoptin	Verapamil	Hypotension, constipation
Nimotop	Nimodipine	Hypotension
Norvasc	Amlodipine	Hypotension
Plendil	Felodipine	Hypotension

Procardia	Nifedipine	Hypotension
Sular	Nisoldipine	Hypotension
Vascor	Bepridil	Hypotension
Verelan	Verapamil	Hypotension, constipation

ACE INHIBITORS – commonly prescribed for hypertension

Brand	Generic	Adverse Effects
Accupril	Quinapril	Hypertension, dry cough, dysgeusia (loss of taste), hyperkalemia (elevated potassium in blood)
Altace	Ramipril	Hypertension, dry cough, dysgeusia, hyperkalemia
Capoten	Captopril	Hypertension, dry cough, dysgeusia, hyperkalemia
Loensin	Benazepril	Hypertension, dry cough, dysgeusia, hyperkalemia
Mavik	Trandolapril	Hypertension, dry cough, dysgeusia, hyperkalemia
Monopril	Fosinopril	Hypertension, dry cough, dysgeusia, hyperkalemia
Prinivil	Lisinopril	Hypertension, dry cough, dysgeusia, hyperkalemia
Vasotec	Enalapril	Hypertension, dry cough, dysgeusia, hyperkalemia
Zestril	Lisinopril	Hypertension, dry cough, dysgeusia, hyperkalemia

ANGIOTENSIN II RECEPTOR ANTAGONISTS – commonly prescribed for hypertension

Brand	Generic	Adverse Effects
Atacand	Candesartan	Hyperkalemia
Avapro	Irbesartan	Hyperkalemia
Cozaar	Losartan	Hyperkalemia
Diovan	Valsartan	Hyperkalemia
Micardis	Telmisartan	Hyperkalemia

VASODILATORS – commonly prescribed for hypertension

Brand	Generic	Adverse Effects
Apresoline	Hydralazine	SLE, tachycardia (high resting heartrate), peripheral neuritis (nerve problems)
Hyperstat	Diazoxide	Edema (excessive fluid accumulation in tissues) tachycardia
Loniten	Minoxidil	Hypertrichosis (excessive hair growth), tachycardia
Rogaine	Minoxidil	Hypertrichosis, tachycardia

ANTIPLATELET AGENTS – these are commonly prescribed to prevent heart strokes

Brand	Generic	Adverse Effects
Aggrenox	Aspirin + Dipyridamole	Bleeding

Ecotrin	Aspirin	GI ulcer, bleeding
Effient	Prasugrel	Bleeding
Persantine	Dipyridamole	Bleeding
Plavix	Clopidogrel	Bleeding
Ticlid	Ticlopidine	Bleeding, agranulocytosis (deficiency of granulocytes in blood)

CORONARY VASODILATORS – commonly prescribed for angina

Brand	Generic	Adverse Effects
Deponit	Nitroglycerine	Lightheadedness, hypotension, headaches
Dilatrate	Isosorbide-dinitrate	Lightheadedness, hypotension, headaches
Imdur	Isosorbide-mononitrate	Lightheadedness, hypotension, headaches
ISMO	Isosorbide-mononitrate	Lightheadedness, hypotension, headaches
Iso-bid	Isosorbide-dinitrate	Lightheadedness, hypotension, headaches
Isordil	Isosorbide-dinitrate	Lightheadedness, hypotension, headaches
Monoket	Isosorbide-mononitrate	Lightheadedness, hypotension, headaches
Nitro-Bid	Nitroglycerine	Lightheadedness, hypotension, headaches
Nitro Dur	Nitroglycerine	Lightheadedness, hypotension, headaches

Nitrolingual	Nitroglycerine	Lightheadedness, hypotension, headaches
Nitrostat	Nitroglycerine	Lightheadedness, hypotension, headaches
Sorbitrate	Isosorbide-dinitrate	Lightheadedness, hypotension, headaches

ASTHMA MEDICATIONS

Brand	Generic	Adverse Effects
Proventil	Albuterol	Headache, nausea, vomiting, diarrhea
Brethine	Terbutaline	Same as above
Maxair	Pirbuterol	Same as above
Serevent	Salmeterol	Same as above
Brovana	Arformoterol	Same as above
Alupent	Metaproterenol	Same as above
Isuprel	Isoprenaline	Same as above
Tornalate	Bitolterol	Same as above
Foradil	Formoterol	Same as above
Perforomist	Formoterol	Same as above
Atrovent	Ipratropium	Same as above
Spriva	Tiotropium	Same as above
Advair	Fluticasone/Salmeterol	Same as above
Symbicort	Budesonide/Formoterol	Same as above
DuoNeb	Albuterol/Ipratropium	Same as above

Combivent	Albuterol/Ipratropium	Same as above
Intal	Cromolyn	Same as above
Nasalcrom	Cromolyn	Same as above
Tilade	Cromolyn	Same as above
AeroBid	Flunisolide	Same as above
Nasalide	Flunisolide	Same as above
Azmacort	Triamcinolone	Same as above
Flonase	Fluticasone	Same as above
Flovent	Fluticasone	Same as above
Asmanex	Mometasone	Same as above
Pulmicort	Budesonide	Same as above
Rhinocort	Budesonide	Same as above
Alvesco	Ciclesonide	Same as above
Accolate	Zafirlukast	Same as above
Singular	Montelukast	Same as above
Zyflo	Zileuton	Same as above
Theo-dur	Theophylline	Same as above

BPH Drugs – commonly prescribed for benign prostatic hyperplasia

Brand	Generic	Adverse Effects
Proscar	Finasteride	Syncope (sudden loss of consciousness), hypotension***
Avodart	Dutasteride	Syncope, hypotension***

Jalyn	Dutasteride/Tamsulosin	Syncope, hypotension
Minipress	Prazosin	Syncope, hypotension
Hytrin	Terazosin	Syncope, hypotension
Cardura	Doxazosin	Syncope, hypotension
Rapaflo	Silodosin	Syncope, hypotension
Uroxatral	Alfuzosin	Syncope, hypotension
Flomax	Tamsulosin	Syncope, hypotension

*** - women who are pregnant or planning to become pregnant should not handle **Proscar, Jalyn** or **Avodart**, as it can cause a birth defect in male children. This includes female pharmacy technicians! These medications are classified under pregnancy category X, meaning they are very harmful to unborn children

COLONY AND ERYTHROCYTE STIMULATORS – commonly prescribed for low erythrocytes

Brand	Generic	Adverse Effects
Neupogen	Filgrastim	Edema, thrombocytopenia
Epogen	Epoetin alfa	Edema, thrombocytopenia
Leukine	Sargramostim	Edema, thrombocytopenia
Neulasta	Pegfilgrastim	Edema, thrombocytopenia

HEMATINIC AGENTS – commonly prescribed for anemia (low red blood cells) and megaloblastic anemia (low red blood cells, larger than normal red blood cells)

Brand	Generic	Adverse Effects

Feosol	Ferrous sulfate	Constipation
Slow Fe	Ferrous sulfate	Constipation
Fer in sol	Ferrous sulfate	Constipation
Ferra TD	Ferrous sulfate	Constipation
Fergon	Ferrous gluconate	Constipation
Simron	Ferrous gluconate	Constipation
Niferex 150	Iron polysaccharide	Constipation
Ferro-folic	Folic Acid	Constipation
InFeD	Iron dextran	Constipation
Vitamin B12	Cyanocobalamin	Constipation

HYPERURICEMIA AND GOUT – commonly prescribed for gout, a form of arthritis

Brand	Generic	Adverse Effects
ColBenemid	Colchicine/Probenecid	Severe diarrhea
Benemid	Probenecid	Hemolytic anemia, hepatic necrosis (severe, rapid hepatitis)
Anturan	Sulfinpyrazone	Blood dyscrasia (low cell count)
Lopourin	Allopurinol	Rash, hepatitis, hematological disorder
Zyloprim	Allopurinol	Rash, hepatitis, hematological disorder

| Uloric | Febuxostat | Liver toxicity |
| Krystexxa | Pegloticase | Anaphylaxis (shock), infusion reactions |

IMMUNOSUPPRESSANTS – commonly prescribed for patients who have had recent transplants

Brand	Generic	Adverse Effects
Imuran	Azathioprine	Organ toxicity, bone marrow suppression, nausea, vomiting
Neoral	Cyclosporin	Organ toxicity, bone marrow suppression, nausea, vomiting
Sandimmune	Cyclosporin	Organ toxicity, bone marrow suppression, nausea, vomiting
Gengraf	Cyclosporin	Organ toxicity, bone marrow suppression, nausea, vomiting
Prograf	Tacrolimus	Organ toxicity, bone marrow suppression, nausea, vomiting
Rapamune	Sirolimus	Organ toxicity, bone marrow suppression, nausea, vomiting
Amevive	Alefacept	Organ toxicity, bone marrow suppression, nausea, vomiting

Zenapax	Daclizumab	Organ toxicity, bone marrow suppression, nausea, vomiting
Ilaris	Canakinumab	Organ toxicity, bone marrow suppression, nausea, vomiting
CellCept	Mycophenolate	Organ toxicity, bone marrow suppression, nausea, vomiting
Myfortic	Mycophenolic acid	Organ toxicity, bone marrow suppression, nausea, vomiting
Arcalyst	Rilonacept	Organ toxicity, bone marrow suppression, nausea, vomiting
Afinitor	Everolimus	Organ toxicity, bone marrow suppression, nausea, vomiting
Zortress	Everolimus	Organ toxicity, bone marrow suppression, nausea, vomiting
Simulect	Basiliximab	Organ toxicity, bone marrow suppression, nausea, vomiting

Drugs That Produce Disulfiram Reactions:

Metronidazole	Chlorpropamide	Cefotetan	Moxalactam
Cefamandole	Tolbutamide	Acetohexamide	Glyburide
Glipizide	Disulfiram		

Drugs that Cause Disulfiram-Like Reactions:

Alcohol	Benadryl	Dioxin	Lanoxicaps

Platelet Aggregation Inhibitors:

Cefamandole	Cefoperazone	Moxalactam	Cefotetan
Plicamycin	Ketorolac	Aspirin	Ticlid
Plavix			

Drugs Requiring a PPI (Patient Package Insert):

Isotretinoin	Oral contraceptives	Isoproterenol	Ticlid
Progesterone	Estrogen	IUD	

Drugs That Shouldn't Be Taken by Pregnant Women

Isotretinoin	Tetracycline	Chloramphenicol	Sulfonamide
Misoprostol	Finasteride	Methimazole	Coumadin
Metronidazole	Valproic Acid	Lithium Carbonate	Alcohol

The 25 Most Common Drugs on the PTCB – Brand and Generic

Brand	Generic
Cymbalta	duloxetine
Geodon	ziprasidone

Celebrex	celecoxib
Advair Diskus	fluticasone/salmeterol
Spiriva	tiotropium
Lyrica	pregabalin
Ambien	zolpidem
TriCor	fenofibrate
Nasonex	mometasone furoate
Namenda	memantine
Levaquin	levofloxacin
Actos	pioglitazone
Cialis	tadalafil
OxyContin	oxycodone
Synthroid	levothyroxine
Nexium	esomeprazole
NovoLog	insulin aspart
Combivent	albuterol/ipratropium
Vytorin	ezetimibe/simvastatin
Provigil	modafinil
Adderall	Amphetamine/dextroamphetamine
Vyvanse	lisdexamfetamine
Zyprexa	olanzapine

Lipitor	atorvastatin
Abilify	aripiprazole

Chapter 4: Maintaining Medication and Inventory Control Systems

This is the second portion of the PTCB exam, and also the second-largest, making up about 25% of what you're expected to know in order to pass the test. Maintaining Medication and Inventory Control Systems is, like the rest of the examination, largely about memorization. Here's a numbered list of everything you'll be tested on when it comes to the big day:

There's a lot less in this section – and the next is even shorter (although there is more material to study.) But just because the test isn't weighted as heavily in this direction doesn't mean that you can skip studying for it. If you end up bombing the calculations or forgetting certain effects of medications in the first part of the test, you'll get a chance to correct course here and still get a passing score. Your pharmacist will also expect you to know this material well!

The Formulary

You remember this from the previous section – a formulary is a list of drugs that a hospital or health care system has approved to be prescribed for patients. The formulary is at the heart of inventory control. If you're in a hospital, it is the master list for what a hospital will keep on hand. If you're in an ambulatory environment (such as a retail pharmacy) the formulary will be specific to plans offered by third-party payers, like insurance companies.

Because each insurance company has its own set of formularies, retail pharmacies don't restrict their inventories as much as hospitals, because the chances they'll need to keep something on hand for patients with dynamic needs is greater.

Ordering Drugs

Depending on where you work, your pharmacy may have someone whose sole job is to purchase pharmaceuticals and maintain the inventory, or they may involve other staff in the job. Either way, ordering pharmaceuticals requires computer systems and Internet technology to manage the processes of procurement, purchase orders and receiving.

As a pharmacy technician, you're most likely going to be responsible for a lot of different processes in this area, such as ordering, receiving, and storing formulary items. There are usually systems in place to make sure that only formulary items are entered into a pharmacy's inventory.

Receiving Drugs

This is one of the most important processes in the pharmacy. If receiving isn't set up correctly, it can lead to all kinds of havoc: Concentration errors, lost or out-of-stock products, you name it. It can lead to delays for patients receiving the medications they really need, and can also increase the overall cost of providing care from your pharmacy.

Because it's so important, the receiving process is usually quite controlled and systematic. The person ordering pharmaceuticals is usually different from the person receiving and storing them. This is especially crucial in the case of handling controlled drugs. The receiving person is usually responsible for:

- Verifying that the number of boxes or plastic crates in an order matches the shipping manifest.
- Verifying the shipment is correct, undamaged and that nothing is missing, and if there are discrepancies or damaged items, marking the shipping manifest as such to protect the pharmacy from financial responsibility

- Ensuring that pharmaceuticals that require refrigeration have been properly transported in cold storage, and are processed first (to get them back in cold storage as quickly as possible.)

- Working within vendor guidelines to handle errors in shipment or the delivery of expired or damaged goods.

- Verifying that the delivered products match up with the purchase order, including names, dosage forms, sizes, brands, quantities and concentrations.

- Verifying that drugs are within the pharmacy's expiration date requirement (most pharmacies require a minimum six months of shelf life on the products that they order.)

- Manually adding information into the system about any product whose bar code does not scan.

- Arranging for any erroneous excess product to be returned to the manufacturer

- Processing controlled substances and filling out the required DEA form 222, then filing with a copy of the invoice and packing slip that came with the controlled substances

- Creating written records of receipt for lost or misplaced purchase orders

Storing Drugs

Once all the medications and equipment have been received, it's up to you to make sure they get stored in a proper manner. There are usually two places to store drugs – one is the pharmacy proper, where drugs are dispensed to patients, and the other is a general storage area away from the dispensation area.

If you're the person in charge of storing drugs, these are your responsibilities:

- Ensuring that stock is properly rotated – removing expired drugs, placing drugs with the longest expiration dates in the back, and moving drugs with the soonest expiration dates to the front. This ensures that expired products aren't used, and helps cut down on waste.

- Ensuring that products are in good condition and stored in the correct area, that liquids/injectables are the proper color and consistency, and that products have no broken seals or anything else unusual in their appearance.

- Ensuring that drugs with similar-sounding names aren't stored too near each other, or are properly labeled with warnings marking them as potential look-alike/sound-alike products.

- Ensuring that drugs with similar package appearances are properly labeled with warnings clearly delineating them. We're all human, and sometimes we don't always read the label if we think we know what the package looks like. The tech has to take special care to guard against this seemingly minor carelessness.

- Ensuring that drugs with similar labels are clearly marked with a warning, to avoid the same problem as above.

- Informing other technicians and staff members about any packages in storage that have similarities and could cause confusion or a potential error.

The Maintenance and Management of Inventory

Inventory management is usually systematized to make sure a pharmacy doesn't have too little or too much product on hand. Sometimes these systems are as simple as an order book where technicians write down what they think the pharmacy needs (this is called "eyeballing it",) sometimes they're complicated economic models, like the Pareto ABC system, and sometimes they're fully automated and computerized.

Pareto ABC System

This is a system in wide use as far as inventory management is concerned – and not just in pharmacies. The theory at the core of it is that managing 20% of the inventory will cover 80% of the costs.

Essentially this system groups together products in the inventory by the average of how much they're worth, and how often they get used. There are three categories: A, B and C. This helps technicians know where the bulk of their efforts concerning inventory control should go. For instance, Group A might be 20% of the items that make up 50% of inventory cost – this would make tightly controlling this group make sense. In this example, Group B might be 30% of the items that make up 30% of the inventory cost and Group C might be the other 50% of items that only make up 20% of the inventory cost. By keeping products in these groupings, technicians know they need to focus most heavily on keeping Group A tightly controlled and groups B and C under a watchful eye, but not as rigidly as Group A.

Par-Level System

This is a manual system that basically sets minimum and maximum levels for inventory and labels them clearly. If you fall below a certain amount of a drug, you'll order more (up to a maximum.) This helps to minimize running out of a particular drug (which could negatively affect patients) or overstocking it (which is an unnecessary expense.) This is a fairly common practice, and is usually managed by a bar code and computer system.

Automated System

More and more, these systems are being implemented at pharmacies around the country. Essentially, a computer tracks each time a drug is dispensed and automatically deducts it from inventory. Once a drug hits a minimum level, the computer will generate an automatic purchase order for it to bring back within its minimum-maximum range. This is a good system, because it doesn't rely on human judgment for basic functions, freeing up technicians' mental and physical resources for more important tasks like assisting patients. However, product availability, changes in contacts with manufacturers, and trends in the patterns of usage of certain drugs over time make it necessary for a human being to be involved in the oversight of any automated system.

Handling Drug Recalls

Occasionally, a manufacturer will <u>recall</u> pharmaceuticals. This may be because of:

- FDA pressure
- Mislabeling
- Lack of potency
- Failure to conform to accepted manufacturing practice
- Contamination
- Any other reason deemed necessary by the manufacturer

The Role of the FDA in Recalls

The FDA regularly evaluates the effects of drugs, and performs analyses of potential health hazards and public risks. If the FDA feels that a drug has become a risk to the public, it informs the manufacturer that it believes the drug should be recalled. It will also give the recall one of three classifications:

1. Class I – This means that continuing use of the medication could result in major harm to a patient, or even death
2. Class II – This means that continuing use of the medication could cause serious adverse effects for a patient or irreversible health consequences

3. Class III – This means that continuing use of the medication isn't likely to cause a serious adverse effect, but a small chance of injury exists

The FDA itself doesn't have the legal authority to recall pharmaceuticals, but the agency can put a lot of public and political pressure on a manufacturer to recall their drugs. In this case, it's considered a *voluntary* recall on the part of the manufacturer, but there isn't much of a history of a manufacturer resisting a request from the FDA to recall their medications, because the FDA has such a large platform to communicate with the American people. The FDA also offers assistance to manufacturers in recalling drugs, and inspects pharmacies' recall logs to ensure they are properly complying with recall procedures.

The Role of the Manufacturer and Distributor in Recalls

If a recall is issued – whether by FDA pressure or the manufacturer's own findings – manufacturers and distributors will send out recall notices to pharmacies indicating:

- The name of the drug being recalled
- The reason the drug is being recalled
- The class of the recall
- The name of the manufacturer
- Any affected lot numbers
- The response pharmacies are required to make
- Instructions for contacting patients who have been dispensed the drug
- Instructions for returning medication to the manufacturer

The Role of the Pharmacy in Recalls

If you receive a recall notice from a manufacturer, your pharmacy will need to take these steps:

- Check the inventory for any recalled product in stock
- Return medication to the manufacturer (or properly destroy it, if the recall calls for that)
- Notify patients and take steps to communicate with them as required by the recall notice
- Document the recall letter and file in the recall log
- Replace affected inventory (if possible) or obtain financial compensation for loss of inventory

Supply and Demand and Medication Shortages

Thankfully, the PTCB won't quiz you on economics, but the old irrefutable law of supply and demand does affect your pharmacy's operations in a big way when it comes to potential shortages.

It's not uncommon that a manufacturer won't be able to supply a medication because of supply and demand. Sometimes the manufacturer can't get raw materials, sometimes there's a problem in the manufacturing process and sometimes they just can't make enough to keep up with demand. In this case, a pharmacist's training will be crucial, because the pharmacist is the only one qualified to discuss alternative therapies with doctors and other prescribing health care professionals.

Counterfeit Drugs

Around the world, there's a growing problem with counterfeit pharmaceuticals. These are chemical compositions that technically have the same elements as many pharmaceuticals dispensed at pharmacies, but they don't meet the same quality, potency and purity standards. Unfortunately, these drugs often get shipped in packages that look identical to those that come from manufacturers.

These are a serious threat to the health of your patients. You need to be aware of the fact that there are unscrupulous chemists in the world making unsafe drugs, and you need to know the methods by which you, as a pharmacy technician, can work to bring this worldwide problem under control.

You can't always get drugs from your regular sources – supply and demand makes sure of that – but occasionally there are alternative distribution channels sanctioned by your pharmacy that you can go to for chemical components when your regular suppliers aren't able to fill your order.

Always check and double-check any alternative drug suppliers licensing information. If they have stock of a product that everyone else is out of, be doubly careful. You need to know what drugs are readily available on the market and which ones the country is experiencing a shortage of, and not be afraid of interrogating an alternative supplier about their supplies and how they're able to stock certain chemicals in a nationwide shortage. Your patients' health and safety depends on your inquisitiveness!

Ordering/Borrowing Drugs

GPOs

Group Purchasing Organizations (GPO) are groups of pharmacies, health systems and hospitals that join together to increase their purchasing power and negotiate lower prices for medications. A GPO usually enters into two kinds of product contracts: Sole-source products, and multisource products.
Sole-source products come from a single manufacturer or supplier, and include brand-name drugs with no competitors on the market. Sometimes, a brand-name drug has competitors on the market, and these sole-source products will be part of something

called a <u>competitive market basket.</u> Multisource products are usually generics that are available from many different manufacturers.

Being in a GPO saves a pharmacy money, staff resources, and affords additional protections against high-cost product shortages.

Direct Purchases

This is when a pharmacy sends a purchase order directly to a manufacturer. This is usually the cheapest way for a pharmacy to obtain needed inventory supplies because there are no third-party handlers or wholesalers. It also has an advantage in that pharmacies aren't required to order drugs at specific times. The disadvantages include a need for a lot of storage and a lot of cash, since manufacturers typically sell wholesale quantities of their drugs, and the need for a lot of staff to prepare a lot of purchase orders for each individual manufacturer from which the pharmacy buys.

Most pharmacies don't buy direct because it's just not advantageous to them in the long run. Usually, a pharmacy will buy from a drug wholesaler.

Drug Wholesalers

Drug wholesalers purchase drugs from many different manufacturers and make them available to GPOs and individual purchasers. When a GPO or individual purchaser agrees to purchase more than 90 percent of its products from a single wholesaler, they've designated that wholesaler as a <u>prime vendor</u>, and they get lower prices because of it. Wholesalers offer a large variety of products and provide emergency support to purchasers; they also design, implement and support inventory systems. Usually, wholesalers bill purchasers three months in advance for the aggregate total of a pharmacy's historical purchases.

The advantages of purchasing through a wholesaler – and designating a prime vendor – are many. Ordering and delivery are faster, staff don't have to spend as much time creating purchase orders and documenting things, data is generated and presented on purchasing trends, and the credit and return process for products is usually drastically simplified compared to direct purchasing.

Borrowing Drugs

Occasionally, pharmacies just run out of supplies, no matter how good their ordering and inventory systems are. No one can foresee sudden spikes in regional demand.

In order to fill empty shelves when the pharmacy really needs supplies, they can borrow drugs from another pharmacy. This is only done in the event of an emergency, and only specially authorized people working in the pharmacy can initiate a borrow or a loan.

Every pharmacy has its own procedures and policies on how to facilitate these transfers, what drugs are able to be transferred, and how to reconcile borrows and loans. Sometimes, especially in the case of controlled substances, a special courier service will need to be called in to transport the drug, along with security. As a pharmacy technician, you need to know these procedures and policies thoroughly to make sure the borrowing and loaning of drugs goes smoothly every time.

Special Products

Usually, you'll use your pharmacy's standard inventory and purchase systems to handle pharmaceuticals. In the case of controlled substances, compounded products, samples, repackaged medications and investigational drugs, there are different systems you'll need to use.

Controlled Substances

The law requires that controlled substances designated as Schedule II need to have their own system for ordering, receiving, storing, dispensing, inventorying, documenting, returning and disposing. Other controlled substances with a lower schedule (III, IV and V) are usually handled through the regular pharmacy systems.

There are two major things you need to know about Schedule II drugs:

1. Ordering and receiving controlled substances means filling out special order forms, and anticipating a slightly longer wait time (usually about three days.)
2. Inventorying and tracking controlled substances are handled in a system called <u>perpetual inventory process.</u> Every dose or packaged unit of a controlled substance needs to be accounted for in your pharmacy continuously.

Depending on your pharmacy and operating environment, you may or may not assist the pharmacist with controlled substances. The Drug Enforcement Agency, also known as the DEA, has many federal regulations governing these drugs to prevent controlled substances from being stolen or lost.

Any time you're handling a controlled substance, you'll need to complete a piece of paperwork called a DEA Form 222, which is triplicate and hand-written. When you order the drugs, you'll fill out the DEA Form 222, and when you receive them, you'll file one of the copies along with the supplier's invoice and the packing slip that came with the medications.

Increasingly, pharmacies have been moving over to a system whereby they order Schedule II controlled substances online, where most of these regulatory systems have been automated in accordance with the law. However, depending on the state you're in, there may be additional laws and regulations concerning receipts, inspection of files and storage.

Chemotherapy

Chemotherapy drugs are hazardous! Because of this, you need to take special care when receiving, handling and storing these drugs. Usually, you'll receive chemotherapy packages separately from other products; when opening and unpacking these, be extra cautious. Any breach in the integrity of the shipping container could be hazardous to your health.

Your pharmacy should have hazardous material protocols in place for incidents such as spills. Be sure and learn it well, for your safety and the safety of your fellow pharmacy workers.

Radiopharmaceuticals

These are usually administered for diagnostic imaging, but some are used to treat certain cancers and thyroid diseases. Radiopharmaceuticals get their name because they're radioactive – making them hazardous to your health! It's important to be exposed to these drugs for as short a duration of time as possible. You need to know your pharmacy's procedures and policies for radiopharmaceuticals well to minimize your risk and the risk to others around you.

Investigational Drugs

Like controlled substances, investigational drugs have their own procedures for ordering, receiving, inventorying and handling. There are usually two kinds of investigational drugs you'll deal with:

1. Drugs used within institution-approved protocols
2. One-time use drugs used on single patients with approval from the FDA and the manufacturer of the medication

In many places, the doctor or prescriber is responsible for ordering the drugs, and the pharmacy is responsible for inventorying it. If you work for a pharmacy that regularly handles investigational drugs, such as a pharmacy for a manufacturer or an academic institution, you may have a section of your pharmacy specifically designated for research. If this is the case, the pharmacist in charge will likely do the ordering, dispensing and inventory management. As a technician, you'll assist pharmacists with their tasks, and will likely handle most of the documentation for the perpetual inventory system.

Restricted Drug Distribution System (RDDS)

The point of the restricted drug distribution system (RDDS) is to make sure high-risk drugs get safely ordered, received, stocked and dispensed.

High-risk drugs include those with serious side effects like birth defects or cardiovascular disruptions. Patients who need these drugs usually have a life-threatening health condition that is riskier to leave untreated than to take these mediations.

If your pharmacy handles restricted drugs, you'll have an RDDS in place. Usually, the RDDS requires:

- The patient's name, date of birth and other information
- The specific indication of the drug
- The dose and quantity the pharmacy intends to dispense
- A patient statement of understanding and agreement to take liability
- The registration of the prescriber
- The registration of the pharmacy

Sometimes, but not always, an RDDS will also require lab results, patient counseling and reimbursement information.

Compounded Medications

Because these are prepared in pharmacies, not in a manufacturer's operating environment, there are strict controls placed on inventorying these drugs. Here's what you need to know regarding compounded medications:

- Compounded medications usually have shorter expiration dates
- Compounded medications need to be tightly monitored for prescribing patterns to ensure the pharmacy doesn't run out
- Patient use needs to be monitored
- Special care needs to be taken when preparing compounds for shipping, because toxic materials are often involved in their production
- Compounds need to be shipped according to specific standards put in place by both the pharmacy and the Department of Transportation.
- Each chemical shipped needs to be accompanied by a Material Safety Data Sheet

Non-Formulary Items

If your pharmacy is stocking something not on the formulary, it probably doesn't have a specific place in your inventorying system. In this case, you'll need a manual system (or special piece of software) to order and keep track of these products.

Medication Samples

Sometimes, drug manufacturers provide samples of a new drug to doctors and physicians free of charge. This is usually happens without a local pharmacy being aware of the transaction.

Pharmacies rarely dispense samples, and if they do, the samples are likely stored outside of the pharmacy (for instance, elsewhere in a hospital.) But if a recall is issued, it's important to communicate that information to physicians in the local area, in case they're still dispensing samples of a recalled product.

If you're called upon to inspect drug sample storage units, you'll need to look for the following things:

- Whether the sample is registered with the pharmacy
- Whether it's stored in a proper quantity
- Whether it's properly labeled
- Whether it's within its expiration date
- Whether it's being stored under proper conditions

Because of the thorny organizational issues involving sample drugs, many hospitals refuse to stock them. If you do work in a pharmacy that handles samples, your pharmacy will have its own policies and procedures in place governing the management of sample inventory.

Returning/Disposing of Drugs

Expired Drugs

Usually, when you're returning a drug to a manufacturer, it's because it has expired. This is usually a simple process involving placing the drugs in their original packaging and sending them back to the manufacturer or wholesaler.

Please note: Sometimes drugs have expiration dates with the day, month and year that they expire. But many manufacturers only list the month and year. If you encounter an expiration date that reads, for example, 03/13, the expiration date of that drug is actually March 1st, 2013. It should not be used any day in the month of March or after.

It's important to return expired drugs so that no one accidentally uses them, and so that your pharmacy can get some money back on its original expenditure. However, if your pharmacy orders items that expire within six months, a lot of wholesalers won't give you full credit back if you return them an expired product. In any case, each wholesaler will have specific documentation you'll need to fill out whenever you're returning an expired drug, whether in paper form or electronic.

Disposing of drugs always needs to be done under the supervision of a pharmacist. There are regulations under the Resource Conservation and Recovery Act – regulated by the Environmental Protection Agency – that some states have recently begun to enforce. These pertain to the way in which expired drugs are disposed of, and if you live in a state that has chosen to enforce these regulations, you may need to become familiar with those requirements. Fear not! If your pharmacy is in one of these states, it will have policies and procedures in place to help you get – and stay – in compliance with the law.

Of course, after a pharmaceutical has been compounded or repackaged, it's no longer able to be returned to the wholesaler, so after their expiration date, they'll have to be properly disposed of. It's important to dispose of drugs properly to prevent the misuse of chemicals and to avoid environmental damage.

The way to dispose of drugs varies, depending on the product. Some drugs you can throw away, and some need hazardous waste service, like cytotoxic products or chemotherapeutic medications. Your pharmacy will have special policies and procedures for handling hazardous wastes, and you need to know them well.

You also can't return chemicals used in the pharmacy laboratory; most of your ingredients used in compounding need to be properly disposed of once they expire.

Controlled substances are not allowed, by law, to be returned to the wholesaler. They have to be properly destroyed, and the destruction needs to be documented on DEA Form 41 (called Registrant's Inventory of Drugs Surrendered) and kept on file for potential inspection by the DEA. Oftentimes, there are companies in the area that are approved by the DEA to destroy controlled substances. If the pharmacy destroys the controlled substances, there is a witness process the DEA requires to ensure the drugs have been destroyed.

Investigational drugs need to be returned to the manufacturer or the sponsor of the study according to the instructions set forth in the investigational study. If an investigational drug becomes unstable or unsterile, *don't destroy them.* It's important that the people conducting the study know the circumstances under which the investigational drug became unusable; the drugs need to be clearly marked as expired and kept alongside the rest of the investigational supply until the entire batch is returned.

If you or another technician makes an error when ordering pharmaceuticals, and you need to return some of them, you'll need to get authorization from the original supplier. There is a law called the Prescription Drug Marketing Act that requires your pharmacy to keep on file the records of authorization and retention for the drugs you've ordered to prevent them from being stolen or lost. Now, medications and supplies that show up as a result of human error are actually fairly common, and both your pharmacy and your supplier should have routine policies and procedures in place to handle it.

Waste Management

Pharmaceutical waste has become a global health issue; trace amounts of medications have found their way into the drinking supply of dozens of U.S. cities, and a lot of them don't get filtered out by municipal water purification plants. Some of these medications are happening because of human urine and feces, but most of it comes from improper waste disposal through sewers and landfills. It's important to properly dispose of all medications in accordance with all applicable laws, rules and regulations to help get a handle on this worldwide problem; the prevalence of hormonal medications, antibiotics and more in the water supply pose a major health threat to people everywhere.

Durable and Non-Durable Equipment and Supplies

There are many kinds of equipment and supplies, but the two this part will cover are durable and non-durable equipment and supplies. Durable equipment and supplies are defined as reusable products ordered by a doctor or other prescriber for use in a patient's home. Non-durable equipment and supplies are designed to be used one time only.

If your pharmacy supplies durable medical equipment and supplies, it means you stock goods such as blood glucose monitoring systems for diabetics, or wheelchairs, or possibly prosthetics for amputees. We'll cover Medicare and Medicaid a little later in the book, but for now it's important for you to know that all pharmacies that supple durable medical equipment need to be accredited to bill Medicare Part B. Medicare covers 80% of durable equipment costs, and the patient is responsible for the other 20%.

Non-durable equipment and supplies are things like needles for insulin injection, examination gloves and diapers – meant to be used one time, then properly disposed of.

Most of what you've learned so far about inventory management applies to durable and non-durable equipment and supplies. However, one thing that might throw you for a loop is a new business model emerging in some places: Rental supplies. Instead of purchasing something outright, some patients have the option of renting durable medical equipment (such as a therapeutic boot for a broken ankle) for the duration of their convalescence. If your pharmacy participates in a rental or lease program, you'll be responsible for handling this equipment, and you might also be responsible for making sure the equipment is thoroughly cleaned, evaluated for integrity, and processed before it's returned to the supplier or rented out to another patient.

Chapter 5: Participating in the Administration and Management of Pharmacy Practice

At last – the third and final portion of the PTCB exam, comprising just 11% of the questions on the test, but incredibly important to know in case you whiff on any of the calculations.

Every state has different pharmacy boards and regulations, but the information in this chapter will give you a general sense of industry best practices and regulations/operations that are standard across the board, nationwide.

Pharmacy Operations

As a pharmacy technician, you need to know each of the regulatory agencies that govern your pharmacy's operations, and all of their regulations, as well. This means standards for scheduled drugs, and how to bill/reimburse patients for treatment.

Regulatory Agencies

This will differ slightly from state to state, but you're most likely to be inspected by:

- The FDA
- The DEA
- The State Pharmacy Board

Accrediting Agencies

Accrediting agencies have a published standard they think pharmacies should operate at, and if a pharmacy is willing to meet that standard, they can receive the accrediting agency's stamp of approval. The most common accrediting agencies are:

- The Joint Commission (TJC, formerly known as JCAHO)

- The American Society of Health-System Pharmacists (ASHP)

- Centers for Medicare and Medicaid Services (CMS)

Getting Ready For Inspection

Regulatory and accrediting agencies will stop by your pharmacy every so often to inspect your operations; they want to be sure that you and your fellow staff are performing up to standard! A typical inspection team will:

- Meet individually with pharmacy staff to ask about how patients are cared for

- Review policy, procedure and turnover manuals

- Review risk management and risk reduction policies and procedures

- Review staff education policies regarding business operations and professional advice

- Review staff recruitment and development policies and procedures

- Collect information regarding the pharmacy's relationship with insurers and third-party billers

- Ensure that all regulatory requirements at the state and national level are required

- Ensure compliance with all applicable laws, statutes and regulations

The P&P

Inspectors will be especially interested in a pharmacy's policies and procedures regarding day-to-day operations. These are usually contained in a large binder called the P&P, which should be easily and readily accessible to all employees, and they are usually developed by the director of a pharmacy, or the pharmacist-in-charge. The P&P generally consists of policies and procedures concerning:

- Proper aseptic technique when compounding IV solutions
- Compounding practices
- Repackaging processes
- Drug allergy monitoring
- Handling of chemotherapy drugs
- Distribution and control of medications
- Ensuring patients receive the correct medication
- Use of investigational medication
- Management of hazardous drugs
- Management of drug expenditures
- Pharmacy budget procedures
- Theft prevention
- Forgery prevention
- Staffing levels
- Billing procedures
- Maintenance of customer accounts
- Inventory control and maintenance
- Medical equipment management

Quality Assurance

Inspectors will also want to know the ways in which your pharmacy assures the quality of its products and services. Quality Assurance (QA) isn't technically required by any regulatory agencies, but there are accrediting agencies that require QA programs to be in place. Here are a few elements you might find in a typical QA program:

- Updating patient records with each visit to the pharmacy to ensure their information is correct
- Using automated drug dispensing systems

- Documentation of inspections of medication storage and dispensation areas
- Using electronic prescription transmission wherever possible
- Completing temperature logs
- Using a bar code system

Federal and State Law

Of course, state law depends on which state you're practicing as a pharmacy technician in, but the major federal laws your pharmacy needs to be in compliance with are:

1. The Food, Drug and Cosmetic Act (FDCA)
2. The Omnibus Budget Reconciliation Act of 1990
3. The Controlled Substances Act
4. The Poison Prevention Packaging Act

Requirements for Labeling Prescriptions

The FDCA has specific rules governing retail prescription labels – they must contain all of the following:

1. The name and address of the dispensing pharmacy
2. The number of the prescription
3. The date the prescription is filled
4. The name of the prescriber
5. The name of the patient
6. Directions for the medication's use
7. Any cautionary statement that comes with the prescription

Remember that medication orders aren't technically prescriptions, so they're not beholden to the same standards. However, each state has its own rules on what the label of a medication order needs to include.

Requirements for Refilling Prescriptions

It differs from state to state, but in general, a patient can refill a prescription as many times as the prescriber allows within a one year time period. If a prescription does not indicate any refills, *no refills are authorized.*

If a patient wants refills, they can ask you to contact a prescriber and obtain their authorization for a refill. This must be done under the supervision of a pharmacist.

The PPPA

The Poison Prevention Packaging Act (PPPA) is a law intended to reduce the number of children who die every year from drug poisoning. This means that drugs now come in child-resistant packages (with a few exceptions) and these child-resistant closures are not allowed to be used for refills.

The PPPA doesn't usually apply to medication orders, but it does apply to any medications the patient goes home with after a stay in the hospital.

If a patient doesn't have children at home, or otherwise is physically unable to open child-resistant containers, the patient or physician can request that the prescription be dispensed in a non-PPPA approved container. You're not required to document these requests, but they do need to be made on a patient-by-patient basis, and can't be issued as a blanket request for all patients of a particular physician or prescriber.

Prescription Drug Information for Patients

When a patient is given medication, they also need to receive some literature called consumer medication information, which is also known as CMI. The FDA also requires that literature called patient package inserts, also known as PPIs, are dispensed with certain drugs like estrogen and birth control medications.

Controlled Substances

The Federal Controlled Substance Act (FCSA) regulates how pharmacies handle controlled substances to prevent them from leaving a therapeutic environment and being misused. The DEA is the regulatory agency that enforces the FCSA.

Any drug that is under the purview of the DEA is called a controlled substance. There are five different schedules of controlled substances, numbered with Roman numerals from I to V.

- *Schedule I* – these are classified as having no medical purpose and a high abuse potential. Drugs in this classification include marijuana and LSD.
- *Schedule II* – these are classified as having legitimate medical purpose and also a high abuse potential. Drugs in this classification include morphine, amphetamine, methamphetamine, cocaine, codeine and opium
- *Schedule III* – these are classified as having a legitimate medical purpose and a medium abuse potential. Drugs in this classification include narcotics with less than 15 mg of hydrocodone per dosage unit, such as Vicodin and OxyContin, and less than 90 mg of codeine per dosage unit. Other drugs in this schedule include ketamine and anabolic steroids.
- *Schedule IV* – these are classified as having a legitimate medical purpose and a lower abuse potential than Schedule III drugs. Drugs in this classification include flurazepam, lorazepam, barbital, meprobamate, sibutramine and clonazepam

- *Schedule V* – these are classified as having a legitimate medical purpose and a lower abuse potential than Schedule IV drugs. Drugs in the classification include cough syrups with small amounts of codeine and drugs containing buprenorphine.

The DEA also maintains two classifications of standalone chemicals that can be used to make controlled substances. There is a List I classification and a List II.

State Boards of Pharmacy

State legislatures make laws that govern the requirements and restrictions for operating a pharmacy within that particular territory. State boards of pharmacy are charged by the law with regulating pharmacy practice. Their purview includes:

- Issuing licenses to pharmacies and pharmacy staff
- Inspecting pharmacies
- Issuing regulations
- Investigating complaints and taking punitive action against pharmacies that violate state pharmacy board regulations

Counseling Requirements

The Omnibus Reconciliation Act of 1990 requires states that receive federal funding to institute programs that improve pharmacy care and save money by educating patients. Part of these programs included a requirement that pharmacies collect certain information from patients, and that the pharmacist counsel the patient when appropriate.

As a pharmacy technician, you'll be involved in collecting information from patients on a regular basis. You should also check with every patient to see if they want counseling from a pharmacist. If they decline, you need to document it.

Keeping Records

The FDCA set out which records pharmacies need to keep, and which ones aren't important. Here's a general list of the kinds of documents a pharmacy is required to keep on file, usually for five years (though it varies from state to state.)

- Purchase invoices
- Records of drug disposition
- Inventory records
- Sales records
- Records regarding theft, loss or other misappropriation of drugs

Your pharmacy will have detailed policies and procedures outlining its procedures for record keeping and how to stay in compliance with the law.

Patient Privacy

The Health Insurance Portability and Accountability Act of 1996, also known as HIPAA, this law was designed, among other things, to strengthen patient privacy. It's critically important that you maintain a patient's confidentiality at all times. Patient records must be kept safe from any unauthorized access, and pharmacy staff are prohibited from discussing a patient's care or medical history unless it's directly relevant to that patient's care. Your pharmacy should also have shredders or a service that picks up documents for disposal.

Communicating Electronically

More and more, electronic devices have pervaded our daily lives – and they're now in wide use in our pharmacies, as well. When you're communicating on the Internet or by fax machine, whether with a patient or a fellow staff member, remember these rules:

- When on the Internet, never ask anyone to provide sensitive information unless you're on a security-encrypted web site.

- Always use a cover sheet when faxing documents – this is required by HIPAA
- Make sure you get some kind of receipt from someone you've faxed documents to in order to ensure they received it and the documents didn't fall into someone else's hands

Billing and Reimbursement

Unfortunately, as a pharmacy technician you'll spend a lot of time dealing with third party payers like insurance companies. That's because the rules and procedures regarding payment are usually quite thorny and change from payer to payer. You'll have to learn rules specific to your state, pharmacy and the available insurance in the area, but the way drugs are billed and reimbursed for generally depend on three factors:

- Who is paying for the drug
- The kind of medication dispensed
- The setting in which the medication is dispensed (inpatient or ambulatory facility)

The most common form of billing and reimbursement is called <u>fee for service</u>, and it works exactly how it sounds. The pharmacy provides a service, and the patient (or their insurer) pays a fee. There is also a model called <u>retrospective payment</u> in which a patient receives the drugs they need, usually pays a copay, and then the pharmacy settles with their third-party payer later. In this case, the third-party payer would reimburse the pharmacy for the care the patient received.

Typically, third-party payers reimburse pharmacies for something called the <u>average wholesale price</u> of a drug, also known as the AWP. The AWP is usually about 20% higher than the <u>wholesale acquisition cost</u> of a drug, which is set by each individual manufacturer. However, neither of these metrics actually measures what a drug costs. In recent years, pharmacies and insurers have started using metrics called the <u>average</u>

sales price (ASP) and average manufacturer price (AMP.) The ASP is determined by reviewing selling price data across the nation, factoring in any discounts and concessions that affect prices, then finding the average. The AMP is the average price that manufacturers charge wholesalers, and it's the metric Medicaid uses to determine what it will reimburse. As of 2010, with the passage of the Patient Protection and Affordable Care Act (also known as health care reform, or Obamacare) the AMP has been established as 175% of the ASP.

Payment for Products and Services

Most patients have some kind of health insurance, but there are still a lot of folks that don't have any. Under the Affordable Care Act, individuals will soon be required to have health insurance or pay a tax penalty, but there may yet still be people without health insurance throughout the next few years.

If a customer is paying cash with no third-party payer reimbursement, they get something called the "usual and customary price." Your pharmacy may call this the "cash price." Most third-party payers reimburse a pharmacy with a formula.

Some manufacturers offer free drugs to patients through something called a PAP, which stands for Patient Assistance Program. PAPs are usually available to low-income patients who don't have insurance and can't afford the medications they need to be healthy. There are also programs called IPAPs (Institutional Patient Assistance Programs) in which manufacturers send bulk amounts of commonly used medications to pharmacies for distribution to any patient in need of them who can't pay out of their own pocket.

There are also a number of state and federal government programs that offer assistance to patients who can't afford their medications.

Private Insurance

Most commonly, people will have private health insurance. They'll either have insurance that is <u>managed care</u>, meaning the patient has a network of providers they have access to, or <u>indemnity</u> insurance, which is more expensive, but gives a patient access to any network they want.

Pharmacy Benefit Managers

Also known as PBMs, these are organizations that take care of the administration of pharmacy benefits for third-party payers. Many PBMs are labor unions, Medicaid/Medicare prescription drug plans, self-insured employers, insurance companies or managed care organizations.

The PBM is responsible for establishing the formulary, which if you'll remember, is the list of goods and services their particular plan is willing to pay for. A PBM also decides whether brand-name drugs should be the first choice, or whether a patient should get a generic, first.

The PBM's most important job is optimizing the clinical and financial performance of a pharmacy benefit, helping to keep the costs down for everyone while keeping the quality of care high.

Processing Private Third-Party Prescriptions

If a patient has a prescription benefit as part of their insurance, they should have an ID card with the information you'll need to collect in order to bill their PBM.

The card should have the following elements:

- The name of the PBM
- The telephone number for the PBM's customer service department

- The patient's name
- The patient's ID number
- The dependent's name (if card belongs to a dependent)
- The BIN#, which references the PBM

Once you've entered that information into the computer and sent off the claim, the PBM will decide to accept or reject it. If the PBM rejects it, they'll send the pharmacy a rejection code; if you receive a rejection code, it's your job to know what it means and how to fix it. Of course, if you can't fix it yourself, you'll have to call the PBM directly and seek assistance.

Processing Public Third-Party Prescriptions

There are two major federal health programs you need to know about: Medicare and Medicaid.

Medicare

This is the program for the elderly, disabled and people with certain diseases. Most Americans qualify for Medicare once they're 65. Medicare has four parts:

- Part A (hospital insurance). This covers inpatient care, nursing facilities, hospice care and some home care. Part A requires a deductible, and coinsurance beyond 60 days of Part A coverage.
- Part B (medical insurance). Medicare Part B is optional medical insurance that people can pay into to acquire outpatient hospital and doctor services, lab tests and durable equipment and supplies.
- Part C (Medicare Advantage plans). This combines Parts A and B, and sometimes has prescription drug benefits like the Medicare Advantage Prescription Drug plan. There are five kinds of Part C plans:

- o Medicare special needs plans
- o Fee-for-service plans
- o Medical savings accounts
- o HMOs
- o PPOs
- Part D (prescription drug coverage). Part D is paid for by CMS and premiums paid by individual patients. It's a voluntary prescription drug benefit administered by PBMs or other Medicare-approved entities. The government requires that nearly every drug in these six categories be covered by Medicare Part D:
  - o HIV/AIDS drugs
  - o Cancer drugs
  - o Immunosuppressant drugs
  - o Antiepileptic drugs
  - o Antidepressant drugs
  - o Antipsychotic drugs

The drugs not covered by Medicare Part D are:

- o Erectile dysfunction drugs
- o Drugs for weight loss/weight gain
- o Barbiturates
- o Benodiazepines
- o Over-the-counter medications

Medicaid

This is a program for medical care that's paid for jointly by state and federal governments. All states participate in Medicaid, which covers three main groups of low-income Americans:

1. Parents and children

2. The elderly

3. The disabled

Patients can receive Medicaid if their income is too low, or they have medical expenses that are greater than a certain amount (which is known as a spend down.) If a patient can receive both Medicaid and Medicare, they are known as dual eligible and Medicare should be the primary payer.

Processing Claims

Inpatient

In a hospital setting, billing for medication orders will be folded into the patient's overall hospital bill for the duration of their stay.

Outpatient

In an outpatient hospital pharmacy, a patient may need to pay for any medications dispensed to them on their way out the door. These are usually considered fee-for-service and are not part of the overall hospital bill.

Medications dispensed in this circumstance need to be billed by quantity using the Healthcare Common Procedure Coding System, also known as the HCPCS code. In order to submit a claim to third-party payer for medication dispensed at an outpatient facility, you'll need to include these pieces of information on the claim:

- The name of the beneficiary
- The Health Insurance Claim Number
- The HCPCS code
- Applicable Common Procedural Terminology Codes
- Diagnosis codes

- National Drug Codes
- Units of service
- Place of service

Retail Pharmacy

Most pharmacy claims come from retail pharmacies and are reimbursed by third-party payers. The process of claiming and reimbursing is known as <u>adjudication</u> and it involves these steps:

1. The pharmacy submits the claim with all necessary information
2. The PBM communicates their proposed reimbursement to the pharmacy. Barring any disagreements...
3. The PBM transmits payment and the claim is settled.

Most pharmacies and PBMs use the NCPDP Telecommunications Standard Format to electronically settle claims. Using this system, you can verify a patient's eligibility, determine whether their prescription is on the PBM's formulary, get information on quantity limits and copays, submit claims and receive payments.

Billing for a Prescription

In order for a claim to go all the way through the system, it needs to include these elements:

- Prescription processor (this is the PBM information on the patient's ID card.)
- BIN (Bank Identification Number)
- PCN (Processor Control Number)
- Pharmacy provider information (your pharmacy will have its own unique set)
- NPI (National Provider Identification)

- NCPDP or NABP code (often called the National Pharmacy Identification Code)
- The patient's eligibility, which is different for each patient, and contains:
  - Their name
  - Their identification number
  - Their group number
  - Their relationship to the plan member (some people are spouses or dependents of individuals holding the plan) and the appropriate code
- Information about the prescription, which is different every time, and contains:
  - The date the prescription was written
  - The date the prescription was filled
  - The NDC (National Drug Code)
  - Usage directions
  - Quantity
  - How many days' supply
  - The number of refills allowed (if any)
  - Product substitution (if any)
  - Physician's signature (electronically, if possible)
  - Physician's NPI number
  - Physician's DEA number

Maintaining Pharmacy Equipment

Your pharmacy should have good policies and procedures in place for maintaining and cleaning pharmacy equipment in order to prevent cross-contamination and equipment breakdown. You need to know these policies and procedures – and the methods by which all of the equipment in the pharmacy needs to be monitored, maintained and cleaned.

Maintaining Non-Sterile Compounding Equipment

After each use, this equipment needs to be cleaned. Each manufacturer will have a maintenance schedule dictating when certain procedures need to be performed to keep the equipment in good working order. There should also be a maintenance log for each piece of equipment. All scales or other devices used to measure weight need to be certified annually to ensure that they're properly calibrated.

Maintaining Sterile Compounding Equipment

This equipment needs to be kept free of all kinds of invisible particles and microorganisms in order to create aseptic, sterile IV solutions. Every day, the equipment should be thoroughly cleaned and sterilized and the floor should be disinfected. The trash should be removed several times a day. If you work in a facility with a Risk Level II or III designation, there will be tougher standards. Your pharmacy will have literature on all the procedures necessary to keep sterile compounding equipment clean and well-maintained.

Biological Safety Cabinet

These store hazardous drugs, and need to be in operation 24/7. They should also be serviced by a certified maintenance person every six months. Your job as a pharmacy technician is to clean and disinfect the BSC on a regular basis with the cleaner recommended by the manufacturer, making sure to cover the work surface, the sidewalls and the back of the cabinet. Never use spray cleaners that use aerosol, as they could damage the HEPA filter.

Repackaging Equipment

This is one of the most common places that cross-contamination occurs, so it's important to use extra caution to make sure this gets cleaned daily.

Medication Errors

You play an important role in making sure that patients always receive the right medication, every time. However, we are all human, and everyone makes mistakes. These are the eleven types of medication errors:

1. Monitoring Errors
2. Deteriorated Drug Errors
3. Wrong Administration Errors
4. Wrong Preparation Errors
5. Wrong Dosage Form Errors
6. Improper Dose Errors
7. Unauthorized Drug Errors
8. Wrong Time Errors
9. Omission Errors
10. Prescribing Errors
11. Compliance Errors

You won't always know which category an error falls into, because it might fall into more than one. Here are the main causes of medication errors:

1. Calculation errors, such as incorrect mathematics or incorrect conversions
2. Abbreviation errors, such as mistaking an O for a zero.
3. High-alert medication errors, when a patient is erroneously given a drug like heparin, insulin or any number of narcotics/opiates.
4. Illegible handwriting

5. Drug name confusion, such as when two drugs sound alike. The ISMP maintains a list of commonly confused drug names here.

Preventing Medication Errors

You may participate in an analysis of your pharmacy's operating systems called an FMEA, or Failure Mode and Effects Analysis. This analysis takes a look at your pharmacy's processes and systems and tries to determine if there are any changes that could be made to reduce medication errors.

One of the most common and effective methods of preventing medication errors is a multiple check system. These come in many different varieties, but they essentially set up a system of redundancies, such as having a pharmacist check a medication prepared by a pharmacy technician, a nurse checking a medication dispensed by the pharmacy, a pharmacist auditing a physician's prescription, and so on.

Your pharmacy should also provide ongoing education and training to pharmacy technicians concerning calculations, procedures, techniques, abbreviations and computer skills in order to reduce the likelihood of mistakes. If your pharmacy is accredited by TJC, they'll be regularly auditing you and your fellow techs to make sure you know your stuff!

When an Error Occurs

Regardless of what happened or who was responsible, you need to notify a pharmacist immediately if there's been a medication error. The pharmacist will conduct an investigation, then make a report to the physician and his or her superiors.

It's important to understand that you as a pharmacy technician can be held personally liable if you make an error with medication out of carelessness, and it results in a patient being harmed.

Practice Questions

In this section, you'll find 100 practice questions designed to simulate the ones you'll find on the PTCB. Study these well, but don't stop here! There are many PTCB practice examinations to be found in libraries and online. These questions will get you started, and will give you a good feel for what you'll encounter on the big day, but the more practice questions you seek out and study, the better off you'll be when it really counts.

1. What is the main difference between a prescription and a medication order?
   a. There is no difference; they are terms used interchangeably for the same thing.
   b. Prescriptions are written only in hospitals and inpatient facilities
   c. Prescriptions are for outpatient facilities, medication orders for inpatient facilities
   d. Medication orders are forms for ordering chemicals

2. What is the definition of a <u>legacy drug?</u>
   a. This is nomenclature for drugs, medications and chemical compounds that don't change, regardless of how pharmaceutical companies have branded them.
   b. This is a trademark used by pharmaceutical companies to identify their particular medication formulations.
   c. It can be purchased without a prescription as long as they're properly labeled for home use.
   d. It must be prescribed by someone with prescription authority, and must be dispensed by legally qualified pharmacies.

3. What does the abbreviation qHS stand for?
   a. Every morning
   b. Every bedtime
   c. Nasogastric
   d. Every evening

4. What does the abbreviation qOD stand for?
   a. Every morning
   b. Every other day
   c. Every afternoon
   d. Twice a day

5. What does the abbreviation DAW mean?
   a. Dispense as written
   b. Dextrose in water
   c. Divide by
   d. Distill always

6. What does the abbreviation NS mean?
   a. Normal saline
   b. Not satisfactory
   c. Nausea
   d. No solution

7. What does the abbreviation a.m. mean?
   a. Take with food
   b. Atlantic meridian
   c. Morning
   d. Left ear

8. What does the abbreviation tbsp. mean?
   a. Tablespoon
   b. Teaspoon
   c. Tincture
   d. Evenings

9. What does the abbreviation g mean?
   a. Glucose
   b. Gram
   c. Gallon
   d. Geodon

10. Which of the following is *not* an element of a medication order?
   a. The name of the patient
   b. The dosage form
   c. The rate and duration of indication of use
   d. The date and time of the order

11. If a patient walks up to your retail pharmacy window and you've served them before, what do you need from them before you can begin processing their prescription?
   a. An identifying piece of information from them, such as their date of birth, address or phone number to confirm their identity
   b. A piece of state or federal identification such as a driver's license, passport, military ID card or Medicare/Medicaid card
   c. Their insurance information or a cash deposit, to be sure they can pay for the prescription before you go to the bother of processing it
   d. Information about significant health conditions they have

12. Which element will you find on a prescription that you won't usually find on a medication order?
   a. The DEA number
   b. The patient's name
   c. The route of administration
   d. The signature and credentials of the prescriber

13. Identify which statement about DEA numbers is *true.*
   a. If the holder of the DEA number is a mid-level practitioner, the first letter will always be "A" or "B."
   b. The second letter of the DEA number is always the last letter of the holder's first name
   c. The seventh number is always the last number of the sum of the odd group and double the sum of the even group
   d. The first, third and fifth numbers are called the even group, and the second, fourth and sixth numbers are called the odd group

14. Which of the following computer error screens does *not* exist?
   a. REFILL TOO SOON
   b. NONFORMULARY/DRUG NOT COVERED
   c. DRUG-FOOD ADVERSE EFFECTS
   d. MISSING/INVALID ID

15. When is it acceptable to use abbreviations on a prescription label?
- a. Never use abbreviations on a prescription label.
- b. It's okay if the prescription is written at an inpatient facility.
- c. It's okay to use only approved, easy-to-understand abbreviations on a prescription label
- d. Because prescription labels are so small, it's important to abbreviate as much as possible in order to fit the maximum amount of information

16. Which regulatory agency is in charge of deciding which medications are classified as "restricted-use?"
- a. The Centers for Disease Control
- b. The Food and Drug Administration
- c. The U.S. Pharmacologists' Pharmacopeia
- d. The United States Drug and Formulary Administration

17. Which of these questions are you *not legally* allowed to answer as a pharmacy technician?
- a. "Is there a chance this drug will conflict with the St. John's Wort supplement I take every day?"
- b. "Is there a generic form of this drug?"
- c. "What size do these capsules come in?"
- d. "How many milliliters are there in an ounce?"

18. Which of these is not a type of reference concerning drug information?
- a. Primary
- b. Tertiary
- c. Secondary
- d. Ancillary

19. When is it okay to consult an Internet resource for drug information to pass to a patient?
- a. Never consult the Internet. You'll never find a more wretched hive of scum and villainy.
- b. Only a pharmacist can judge the quality and accuracy of the information in an Internet resource
- c. It's fine to repeat anything you've read on the Internet. If it wasn't true, they wouldn't allow it to be published.
- d. When you know the Internet resource is high-quality, from a trusted source, accurate and completely up-to-date.

20. What are the compounder's responsibilities?
   a. The compounder is in charge of most elements of the compounding process, including ensuring that all personnel have at least a modicum of understanding when it comes to chemistry.
   b. The compounder is in charge of (and accountable for) every element of the compounding process, including ensuring that all personnel are trained properly.
   c. The compounder is in charge only of the finished product; the pharmacy technician is responsible for the acquisition, storage and handling of individual chemical components.
   d. The compounder is responsible for the acquisition, storage and handling of individual components prior to the compounding process.

21. What piece of equipment is a square tile, made of glass, that is used to make creams, topical solutions and ointments?
   a. Pill tile
   b. Ointment Slab
   c. Ointment Paper
   d. Both a and b are correct

22. What is the name of the process of reducing a large substance into particles?
   a. Comminution
   b. Trituration
   c. Grinding
   d. None of the above

23. What is the name of the process of reducing the particle size of a chemical compound by grinding with a mortar and pestle?
   a. Levitation
   b. Desiccation
   c. Trituration
   d. None of the above

24. Which of the following is *not* one of the disadvantages of IV medicine?
   a. It's painful for patients
   b. It can cause extravasation, which is when the needle goes straight through a patient's vein.
   c. It can cause a patient to become dehydrated quickly
   d. It can cause phlebitis, an irritation or swelling of the vein

25. If a doctor requests an IV drip of half-normal saline for a patient, what should the ratio of sodium chloride to water be?
    a. 0.45g NaCl in 100 mL of water
    b. D10 in 100 mL of water
    c. 0.225g NaCl in 100 mL of water
    d. D5NS in 0.9% NaCl

26. Where is the critical area of the LAFW?
    a. The HEPA filter, which nothing should ever come in contact with
    b. The flow of air between the HEPA filter and the sterile workspace
    c. Six inches from the top and bottom of the laminar hood
    d. Twelve inches from the top and bottom of the laminar hood

27. Most vials, ampules and syringes used for solution storage are typically made of:
    a. Glass, because it keeps chemical compounds less stable over time, and it's important to let chemicals change and evolve so that they reach maximum potency
    b. Glass, because it keeps chemical compounds more stable over time than plastic
    c. Plastic, because it keeps chemical compounds less stable over time, and it's important to let chemicals change and evolve so that they reach maximum potency
    d. Plastic, because it keeps chemical compounds more stable over time than glass

28. Which of the following is not an element of a proper IV solution label?
    a. The sequence number of the bag or bottle, if necessary
    b. The prescribed flow rate (ml/hour)
    c. The BSA of the patient to whom the IV is being administered
    d. The initials of the person who prepared the solution, and the initials of the person who checked it

29. What is in the FDA's *Orange Book*?
    a. References and links for pharmacy technicians
    b. Approved drugs, therapeutic and biological equivalents
    c. Drug information for physicians and other prescribers
    d. There is no such thing

30. The Roman numeral IX is equal to what Arabic numeral?

     a. 1
     b. 5
     c. 4
     d. 9

31. Add these fractions:

$$\frac{1}{3} + \frac{1}{6} = \, ?$$

     a. 1/3
     b. 1/6
     c. 1/2
     d. 1/9

32. Subtract these fractions:

$$\frac{1}{2} - \frac{1}{3} = \, ?$$

     a. 1/6
     b. 1/9
     c. 1/2
     d. 1/3

33. Multiply these fractions:

$$\frac{4}{5} \times \frac{3}{8} = \, ?$$

     a. 12/40
     b. 3/10
     c. 6/20
     d. 3/20

34. Divide these fractions:

$$\frac{4}{5} \times \frac{3}{8} = \, ?$$

     a. 12/40
     b. 32/15
     c. 15/32
     d. 2 and 2/15

35. Convert this fraction to a decimal: $\dfrac{4}{5}$

    a. 0.4
    b. .8
    c. .4
    d. 0.8

36. Convert 75% to a fraction:

    a. 2/3
    b. 2/4
    c. 1/4
    d. 3/4

37. What is the means of these two ratios? $\dfrac{5 \text{ mg}}{10 \text{ mL}} = \dfrac{???}{100 \text{ mL}}$

    a. 5
    b. 50
    c. 100
    d. 10

38. Which of these measurement systems is the most common you'll encounter in a pharmacy?

    a. The Household System
    b. The Avoirdupois System
    c. The Metric System
    d. Centigrade

39. How many milliliters are in a fluid ounce?

    a. 30
    b. 15
    c. 5
    d. 473

40. If the temperature outside is 50 degrees Fahrenheit, what temperature is it in Celsius?

    a. 21
    b. 10
    c. 15
    d. 50

41. If the temperature outside is 25 degrees Celsius, what temperature is it in Fahrenheit?

    a. 70
    b. 80
    c. 77
    d. 87

42. If you have a solution of 19% dextrose in 400 mL of water, how many grams of dextrose are in the solution?

    a. 55 grams
    b. 70 grams
    c. 75 grams
    d. 50 grams

43. If the clock reads 7:35 PM, what is that in military time (the 24 hour clock?)

    a. 0735
    b. 0935
    c. 1735
    d. 1935

44. What is the BSA of a patient who is 5'4" and 105 pounds?

    a. 1.8352929
    b. 1.4679700
    c. 1.3422371
    d. 2.0116579

45. If 50 tablets costs $28.00, how much does 25 tablets cost?

    a. $14.00
    b. $15.00
    c. $16.00
    d. $20.00

46. If a doctor writes a prescription for 3 mg /1 kg of body weight for a patient that weighs 240 pounds, how many milligrams of medication do they need daily?
   a. 109 mg
   b. 327 mg
   c. 309 mg
   d. 127 mg

47. If a doctor writes a prescription for 200 mL of a solution with a concentration of 1:1000, and you know that 1,000 mL of the solution has 30 grams of medication in it, how much medication should 200 mL of solution have in it?
   a. 30
   b. 100
   c. 6
   d. 12

48. If a patient is receiving 100 mL of a solution intravenously over an hour, how many mL do they receive in 22 minutes?
   a. 36.67
   b. 37.33
   c. 35.67
   d. 36.33

49. You receive a medication order for 200 mg/m^2 of chemotherapy solution over 3 minutes. Your patient has a BSA of 1.8352929. How many mg of the drug should you prepare?
   a. 300
   b. 368
   c. 200
   d. 268

50. Find the mean of these four numbers: 1, 3, 5, 7
   a. 4
   b. 5
   c. 6
   d. 7

51. Find the median of these six numbers: 20, 22, 24, 26, 28, 30
  a. 24
  b. 26
  c. 25
  d. 20

52. How much does a liter of ethanol, which has a specific gravity of 0.787, weigh compared to a liter of water?
  a. A trick question; they weigh the same
  b. 213 milligrams less than water
  c. 213 grams less than water
  d. None of the above

53. What are the class of drugs known as ACE inhibitors commonly prescribed for?
  a. Hypertension
  b. Asthma
  c. Anemia
  d. Pain Management

54. What is the generic name of the drug Procanbid?
  a. Atenolol
  b. Metoprolol
  c. Propranolol
  d. Procainamide

55. What is the brand name of the drug dutasteride?
  a. Minipress
  b. Rapaflo
  c. Flomax
  d. Avodart

56. What are the adverse effects of the drug Apresoline?
  a. Hyperkalemia
  b. SLE, tachycardia, peripheral neuritis
  c. Edema, tachycardia
  d. SLE, GI ulcer, hypertrichosis

57. What is the generic name of the drug Advair?
    a. Fluticasone/Salmeterol
    b. Albuterol
    c. Albuterol/Ipratropium
    d. Formoterol

58. What is the brand name of the drug irbesartan?
    a. Cozaar
    b. Diovan
    c. Avapro
    d. Atacand

59. What is the generic name of the drug Spiriva?
    a. Fluticasone
    b. Ziprasidone
    c. Tiotropium
    d. Oxycodone

60. What is the brand name of the drug amphetamine/dextroamphetamine?
    a. Ritalin
    b. Adderall
    c. Geodon
    d. Abilify

61. What is the generic name of the drug Lipitor?
    a. Atorvastatin
    b. Duloxetine
    c. Ziprasidone
    d. Levothyroxine

62. What is the brand name of the drug oxycodone?
    a. Ambien
    b. OxyContin
    c. Cymbalta
    d. Provigil

63. Which of these is *not* a common side effect of asthma medications?
   a. Thrombocytosis
   b. Headache
   c. Nausea
   d. Vomiting

64. What is gout?
   a. Hepatic necrosis
   b. A blood disease
   c. A form of arthritis
   d. An immunosuppressant drug

65. Why shouldn't women who are pregnant or could become pregnant handle the drugs Proscar, Jalyn or Avodart?
   a. They contain progesterone
   b. They can cause high birth weight
   c. They can cause birth defects in male children
   d. It's perfectly safe for women to handle these drugs

66. Which of these drugs does *not* require a PPI (Patient Package Insert?)
   a. Hydrocodone
   b. Ticlid
   c. Oral contraceptives
   d. Isotretinoin

67. Which of the following is *not* a commonly used inventory method?
   a. Pareto ABC system
   b. The "eyeball" system
   c. Par-Level system
   d. Automated method

68. If a drug's expiration date reads 06/14, what is the actual expiration date?
   a. May 31st, 2014
   b. June 15th, 2014
   c. June 1st, 2014
   d. June 30th, 2014

69. In the event of a drug recall, what should you do?
    a. The manufacturer will specify the course of action your pharmacy needs to take
    b. Call all patients immediately and tell them to stop taking medication
    c. Call 911
    d. Let the pharmacist handle it; it's their job

70. What does GPO stand for?
    a. Great Pharmacy Organization
    b. Good Practices Omnibus
    c. Group Pharmacy Organization
    d. None of the above

71. Under what circumstances may a compounded drug be returned to the supplier?
    a. Only if it is still made up of individual components and hasn't been mixed yet
    b. Only if the compound is on the formulary
    c. Only if all the ingredients in the mix have passed their expiration date
    d. It's never acceptable to return a compounded drug

72. What is an example of non-durable medical supplies?
    a. Insulin needles
    b. Colostomy bags
    c. Wheelchairs
    d. Crutches

73. Which of the following is *not* a federal regulatory agency?
    a. Drug Enforcement Agency
    b. Food and Drug Administration
    c. Center for Disease Control
    d. National Institute for Health

74. What does P&P stand for?
    a. Practices and procedures
    b. Policies and procedures
    c. Procedures and policies
    d. Procedures and practices

75. Which of the following is a Schedule II drug?
    a. Cough syrup with codeine
    b. Vicodin
    c. Ketamine
    d. Amphetamine

76. Which schedule is the drug OxyContin classified under?
    a. Schedule I
    b. Schedule III
    c. Schedule II
    d. Schedule IV

77. Which of the following are responsibilities of the state pharmacy board?
    a. Enforcing rules, regulations and laws developed by state legislatures
    b. Licensing pharmacies and pharmacy staff
    c. Both a and b
    d. Neither a nor b

78. What is the standard format for electronically settling claims?
    a. The Internet
    b. The NCPDP Telecommunications System
    c. The NCPDP Telecommunications Standard Format
    d. The NCPDP Online Standard System

79. Which of the following is *not* a federal law that applies to pharmacy practice?
    a. The Food, Drug and Cosmetic Act (FDCA)
    b. The Omnibus Budget Reconciliation Act of 1990
    c. The Controlled Substances Act
    d. All of these federal laws apply to pharmacy practice

80. Which law required childproof packaging for prescriptions?
    a. The Omnibus Budget Reconciliation Act of 1990
    b. The Drug Listing Act
    c. The Environmental Protection Act
    d. The Poison Prevention Packaging Act

81. Which of the following is *not* a common medication error?
    a. Monitoring Error
    b. Quality Error
    c. Dosage Form Error
    d. Administration Error

82. Which of the following is a common cause of medication errors?
    a. Negligence Error
    b. Abbreviation Error
    c. Compounding Error
    d. Incompetency Error

83. What does FMEA stand for?
    a. Food, Medication and Education Agency
    b. Failure Mark and Effects Analysis
    c. Failure Mode and Effects Analysis
    d. Failure Mode and Effects Association

84. What is the first thing you should do in the event of a medication error?
    a. Try to fix it if it's within your power
    b. Call the patient and tell them to discontinue use of the medication immediately
    c. Fill out appropriate paperwork for the FDA and DEA and report the incident
    d. Tell the pharmacist

85. Which of these drugs is commonly prescribed for congestive heart failure?
    a. Ethmozine
    b. Cerebyx
    c. Primacor
    d. None of these are commonly prescribed for congestive heart failure

86. Which of these drugs is considered an antiarrhythmic agent?
    a. Cordarone
    b. Tambocor
    c. Dilantin
    d. All of these are antiarrhythmic agents

87. What is the main adverse side effect of drugs in the beta-blocker classification?
   a. Bradycardia
   b. Hemolytic Anemia
   c. Hypertension
   d. Hepatitis

88. Which of these drugs is *not* commonly prescribed for hypertension?
   a. Ticlid
   b. Apresoline
   c. Avapro
   d. Cozaar

89. Which of these drugs is *not* an asthma medication?
   a. Alupent
   b. Tornalate
   c. Imdur
   d. Spriva

90. What are the main adverse side effects of asthma medication?
   a. Tachycardia
   b. Hypotension, bleeding
   c. Headache, nausea, vomiting, diarrhea
   d. Constipation, edema

91. What is the class of drugs most commonly prescribed to patients with recent organ transplants?
   a. Beta Blockers
   b. Immunosuppressants
   c. Hemanitic agents
   d. Coronary Vasodilators

92. What is the class of drugs most commonly prescribed to patients with angina?
   a. Antidepressants
   b. Coronary Vasodilators
   c. Antiplatelet agents
   d. Vasodilators

93. Which of the following produces a serious reaction with disulfiram?
- a. Metronidazole
- b. Moxalactam
- c. Glyburide
- d. All of the above

94. Medications that are very harmful to unborn children are in pregnancy category ___:
- a. X
- b. Y
- c. Z
- d. None of the above

95. Which of the following is not a colony/erythrocyte stimulator?
- a. Neupogen
- b. Epogen
- c. Leukine
- d. Cardura

96. Which of the following groups of low-income Americans are covered under Medicaid?
- a. Parents and children
- b. The elderly
- c. The disabled
- d. All of the above

97. Which part of Medicare covers hospital insurance?
- a. Part A
- b. Part B
- c. Part C
- d. Part D

98. Which part of Medicare is prescription drug coverage?
- a. Part A
- b. Part B
- c. Part C
- d. Part D

99. The acronym PBM stands for:
   a. Pharmacy Billing Managers
   b. Pharmaceutical Benefis of Medicare
   c. Pharmacy Benefit Manager
   d. Pharmacy Bills Medicaid

100. Which drugs are *not* covered under Medicare Part D?
   a. HIV/AIDS drugs
   b. Antipsychotic drugs
   c. Barbiturates
   d. Immunosuppressant drugs

Question	Answer	Question	Answer
1	c	26	b
2	d	27	b
3	b	28	c
4	b	29	d
5	a	30	b
6	a	31	c
7	c	32	a
8	a	33	b
9	b	34	d
10	c	35	d
11	a	36	d
12	a	37	d
13	c	38	c
14	c	39	a
15	a	40	b
16	b	41	c
17	a	42	a
18	d	43	d

19	d	44	b
20	b	45	a
21	d	46	b
22	a	47	c
23	c	48	a
24	c	49	b
25	a	50	a

Question	Answer	Question	Answer
51	d	76	b
52	d	77	c
53	a	78	c
54	d	79	d
55	d	80	d
56	b	81	b
57	a	82	b
58	c	83	c
59	c	84	d
60	b	85	c
61	a	86	d
62	b	87	a
63	a	88	a
64	c	89	c
65	c	90	c
66	a	91	b
67	b	92	b
68	c	93	d

69	a	94	a
70	d	95	d
71	d	96	d
72	a	97	a
73	d	98	d
74	b	99	c
75	d	100	c

Made in the USA
San Bernardino, CA
26 July 2016